Write! Mathematics

Multiple Intelligences & Cooperative Learning Writing Activities

Virginia DeBolt

Kagan

COOPERATIVE LEARNING

Kagan Cooperative Learning
1160 Calle Cordillera
San Clemente, CA 92673
1(800) WEE CO-OP
www.KaganCoopLearn.com

ISBN: 1-879097-38-9

Table of Contents

Virginia DeBolt: *Write! Mathematics*
Kagan Cooperative Learning • 1 (800) WEE CO-OP

I

Table of Contents

Journal Topic Chart

You will find Journal Topics on pages:

27, 63, 71

Virginia DeBolt: *Write! Mathematics*
Kagan Cooperative Learning • 1 (800) WEE CO-OP

II

Chart of Structures

	Basic Description	See Also Activities
Do-What-I-Write	106	1
Find-Someone-Who	107	12
Formations	108	7
4S Brainstorming	109	2
Jigsaw	110	16, 20
Pair Discussion	111	7
Pair Project	111	8, 22, 27, 29, 35
Pairs Present	112	8, 29, 35
RallyTable	112	4, 23
RoundRobin	113	3, 5, 6, 10, 11, 13, 14, 15, 18, 21, 23, 25, 26, 28, 30, 31, 32, 34, 36
RoundTable	114	6
Send-A-Problem	115	6, 30
Simultaneous Chalkboard Share	116	3, 24, 32
Simultaneous RoundTable	117	34
Team Discussion	117	3, 10
Team Project	118	3, 4, 19, 32, 33
Team Sort	119	2, 27
Teams Present	120	4, 19, 21, 27, 33
Team Word Web	121	21
ThinkPad Brainstorming	122	11, 13, 27
Think-Pair-Share	123	15, 26
Think-Write-Pair-Share	124	9
Think-Write-RoundRobin	125	17, 24, 36
Write-What-I-Do	126	1

Acknowledgements

Many people at Kagan Cooperative Learning worked with me to bring this book to completion. Thank you to Spencer Kagan for his continuing support and assistance, to Miguel Kagan for overseeing the details of putting this book into its present form, to Karen Schumacher and Catherine Hurlbert for formatting the book, to Celso Rodriguez for creating the art, and to Jeanne Stone who contributed an invaluable critique and served as editor.

Thanks to my mathematical teammate at Murchison Middle School, Anita Sybesma, who gave me the women in mathematics idea for Activity 8, as well as ongoing support and math minded ideas.

IV

Virginia DeBolt: *Write! Mathematics*
Kagan Cooperative Learning • 1 (800) WEE CO-OP

Integrating Writing and Mathematics

"Countless careers rise or fall on the ability or inability of employees to state a set of facts, summarize a meeting or present an idea coherently."

—William Zinsser

Today's teachers are encouraged to include writing in all the subject areas, including mathematics. Writing during math or in the math classroom may feel foreign at first. Numbers and symbols are perceived to be the language of math. However, integrating writing in math enhances and improves students' understanding of math. Writing is a tool for learning in math as surely as a compass or a calculator. Teachers can use writing as part of daily instruction. Students can use writing in math, not as a novelist or poet would use writing, but the way a mathematician would use writing.

To write is to compose. To compose well is to comprehend. Writing is not speaking, where we hope that the, ahh, listeners, like, you know, get it. Writing demands careful word choice, clear thinking, complete communication. The physical act of writing takes longer than thinking or speaking, and so seems to allow the brain time for the discoveries and connections writers often make while writing. Professional writers, when asked to explain why they write, often answer that they write to find out what they're thinking, what they know and what it means. As students write, they develop their knowledge of a subject. They discover, organize, classify, connect and evaluate information.

Integrating writing and math moves students beyond the basic facts of math. Writing allows students to look critically and creatively at math, enriching students' understanding and

Writing to Learn	vs.	**Reading to Learn**
What do you have to say?		What did they have to say?
Be active. Do it.		Sit still. Pay attention.
Student chooses the words.		Teacher chooses the words.
Productive. Output.		Consumptive. Input.

Virginia DeBolt: *Write! Mathematics*
Kagan Cooperative Learning • 1 (800) WEE CO-OP

1

appreciation of math. By writing about math, students are doing the work of true math; learning becomes more real and more meaningful. As you integrate writing and math, think of it as an enhancement to teaching math rather than as one more thing to cram into an already crowded curriculum.

Indeed, writing is a terrific tool for teaching math as well as the other disciplines, but it is more than that. Writing is a life skill, highly valued by society. Writing is everywhere. Every aspect of human endeavor needs writing about— how else would we pass along the information? The box below is a partial list of things people write or write about. Notice how diverse the writings are.

This list is not at all complete. Wander through the nonfiction stacks in your library. People write about everything. Most writing today is nonfiction, and the need for nonfiction writers continues to grow. Expanding technology in an information age demands it. Nonfiction has never been so important. We are building our national future on information and writers are in demand to explain it. We live in a wired world where communication is essential. Writing across the curriculum gives students the ability to think and communicate today and tomorrow.

So, What Do I Need to Know About Writing?

Enough about the rationale for integrating writing. You're probably reading this book now because you're already convinced about the value of writing. So what do you need to know? The first thing you and your students should know about writing is that there are 10 rules to writing that

What We Write About

- advertisements
- agendas
- animal medicine
- animals
- annotated calendars
- art
- autobiographies
- awards and inscriptions
- biographies
- biology
- business
- captions and labels
- cartoons
- case studies

- chemistry
- coin new words
- collecting
- computer programs
- concerts
- constellations
- contest entries
- dance
- diaries and journals
- drug abuse
- e mail
- economics
- editorials and opinions
- essays

- eulogies
- fashion
- features
- field guides
- field journals
- film
- folk remedies
- folk traditions
- folklore
- foreign language journaling
- forms
- games and puzzles
- geography
- history

Virginia DeBolt: *Write! Mathematics*
Kagan Cooperative Learning • 1 (800) WEE CO-OP

2

10 Rules for Writers

1. Write.
2. Write.
3. Write Often.
4. Write about anything.
5. Write about everything.
6. Write about what you see.
7. Write about what you learn.
8. Write about what you think.
9. Write about what you read.
10. WRITE!

The Writing Process

are absolutely critical. See the 10 Rules at left. These 10 rules are a way to emphasize that the road to becoming a better writer (and mathematician) is to write, write, and write some more! Use these 10 rules as a handout or overhead as you describe the use of writing to your students (see page 14).

The next thing about writing you and your students should know is that writing is considered a process—the Writing Process. This process includes prewriting, revising, editing, proofreading and publishing. Publishing is not necessarily a "publication." Publishing could be reading work aloud to the class, posting work on a bulletin board, polishing an essay to turn in to the teacher or other types of sharing. Teaching students to move about in the process of writing is often considered as important as the final written product.

The writing process is not linear. It is a process. At any point, students can confer, evaluate, and rewrite. For that reason, the writing process is put in a wheel with Conferring/Evaluating/Rewriting in the center of the wheel (see page 15).

The activities in this book focus heavily on the prewriting and writing stages of the process. We've already covered writing, what's so important about prewriting? It's the time when concepts form, vocabulary develops, ideas grow from the synergy of interaction with other students. Prewriting is a social act. Students talk, banter, give and receive feedback. Prewriting develops the readiness to write. Prewriting primes the pump from which the writing will pour.

In the activities in this book, students discuss, plan, outline and brainstorm cooperatively before

What We Write About

- humor
- instructions and advice
- interactive media
- interviews
- learning logs
- lists and notes
- literature
- medicine
- memoirs
- memoranda and messages
- mottoes and slogans
- music
- mythology
- nature

- news stories
- office business
- oral histories
- parodies
- petitions
- philosophy
- physics
- public notices
- recipes
- reports of current events
- research reports
- resumes and cover letters
- reviews
- rules and regulations

- scrapbooks
- simulations
- song lyrics
- sports
- technology
- telegrams
- textbooks
- thumbnail sketches
- time capsule lists
- travel

Virginia DeBolt: *Write! Mathematics*
Kagan Cooperative Learning • 1 (800) WEE CO-OP

3

they actually do any writing. The reason is because prewriting makes writing easier and better. Writers will tell you that they are always writing. A composition of words swirls inside the brain no matter what else a writer might appear to be doing. When a writer sits down to write, it may seem that the words flow easily, when actually considerable time was spent on the words already.

Since most students will not be rehearsing compositions during their spare moments, you can improve the quality of what students write by providing ample time for prewriting activities. As a rule of thumb, the more time you allow for prewriting, the better the writing will be. Therefore, if you draw from only one aspect of the writing process, let it be prewriting.

But prewriting and writing are not the whole story for integrating writing and math. Consider these examples: *Lives of a Cell* by Lewis Thomas, *Silent Spring* by Rachel Carson, *Voyage of the Beagle* by Charles Darwin, *The Immense Journey* by Loren Eisley. These books contain some of the most powerful and beautiful language ever written. Like all good writing, these books were not just written. They were revised, proofread, carefully edited, and finally published, to be shared with others.

Sharing and publishing are extremely important parts of the writing process, not to be

overlooked. By sharing, students can learn from each other what good writing looks and sounds like. Since the writing is about math, students become their own math teachers as they share their learning, connections and reflections.

Many activities include a sharing component. You can easily have students read any of their writing to a partner, to teammates, or even to the entire class. Students can also share their writing by exchanging papers or by posting their papers in a location where classmates can read them. Sharing and publishing make writing a learning experience not only for the writer, but for the recipient as well.

Peer Editing and Conferencing

The math writing activities in this book focus primarily on using writing as a means to teach math. The emphasis is more on the content than the writing itself. However, with a little work, any writing assignment can be easily turned into a polished work of art. What do you do when students need to revise, proofread and edit? Let students help each other. Establish small groups for peer editing and conferencing.

Students offer each other valuable ideas about writing. Since students identify with the words they write and can be

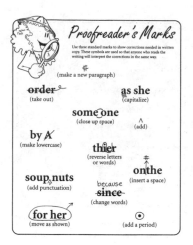

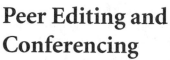

4

Virginia DeBolt: *Write! Mathematics*
Kagan Cooperative Learning • 1 (800) WEE CO-OP

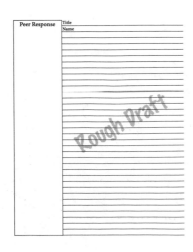

eternally wounded by thoughtless critical comments, your task is to keep the conferences positive. Because students can sometimes be masters of the outspoken insult, it helps to establish a few basic rules for peer conferences, such as:

• Begin with positive comments about what is good in the writing.

• Ask questions that help the writer discover ways to change writing for the better, like:

"I don't understand, could you explain this part a little more?"

"Do you think it would help to change the order of these paragraphs?"

"Would you like for me to underline the words I think you've spelled wrong?"

• Remember that the writer is the final judge of how the writing should be changed

As a peer conference technique, teaching students to ask questions about another's writing works well. The questions become an indicator of where the writing needs to be changed and improved. There are fewer hurt feelings and arguments because the writers learn what doesn't work in their writing without hearing comments such as, "That third paragraph really stinks—throw it out."

It will help students maintain a positive attitude toward each other if you brainstorm with them to develop a list of ways to say things

that help without hurt or insult. Ask them, "How would you like to be told that your writing was disorganized or unclear?" Post their ideas for easy viewing.

In the back of this chapter, you will find a number of forms that will be helpful for peer editing and conferencing. On page 16, there is a Proofreader's Marks form. Have students use these standard marks as they edit each other's papers. For consistency, use them yourself as you edit students' papers.

On page 17 there are gambit cards for students to use in peer conferences. These gambit cards are sentence starters for students as they have peer conferences. They direct the conference and promote a positive tone.

The Peer Conference Response Form is another form helpful for peer conferences, see page 18. Have students fill out their response form before the peer conference, then students go over their comments together.

Page 19 is a Peer Response Form. Students write in the lined space provided. When done, they give it to a peer to respond to the writing in the left margin. They then meet to go over the responses.

What About Grading?

A writing assignment will sink into quicksand if students think they won't be graded. The type of grading you do largely depends on

Virginia DeBolt: *Write! Mathematics*
Kagan Cooperative Learning • 1 (800) WEE CO-OP

5

the type and frequency of writing assignments students do. I suggest an on-going, long-term approach to writing and grading, using writing journals and a writing portfolio. We will look at both journals and portfolios in depth after some general comments on grading.

The first comment on grading is: Don't make grading too labor-intensive for yourself to limit the frequency and volume of student writing. The more students write, the more they learn. More writing also means more grading and more work for you, right? Not necessarily. If you have unlimited time and energy, grade and respond to every writing assignment. If not, grade everything but don't read everything. Yes, grade everything but don't read everything. Students need to know that everything they write might be read, but that doesn't mean you have to read everything. We'll examine this idea in more detail in the sections on journals and portfolios.

The second general comment on grading is: Align your grading practices with the type of writing students do. Glance through the journal topics and activities in this book. You will see a range of writing assignments. You should use a different grading approach depending on the type of writing.

Writing assignments that check for understanding should be turned in for immediate response while the topic is still fresh. Elaborate writing assignments like reports and final papers require individual attention, feedback and usually impact a student's course grade. With most other activities and journal writings, the process of writing and sharing is more important than the evaluation. Students can save these assignments for periodic journal and portfolio checks.

A multipronged approach to grading allows the teacher to hold students accountable for even the most frequent writing assignments, yet at the same time, makes it unnecessary for the teacher to read every word the student writes.

Writing Journals

Some writing might be done in a daily journal. A spiral-bound notebook is a nice way to keep all journal writing assignments together.

Good journal topics are reusable.
- Write for five minutes about yesterday's homework.
- Tell everything you learned about _____ today.
- What did you miss on the test? Do you know it now?
- Summarize last night's assignment.
- We are beginning a new chapter. Write everything you already know about it. Tell what you want to know about it.

Virginia DeBolt: *Write! Mathematics*
Kagan Cooperative Learning • 1 (800) WEE CO-OP

- Write about the hardest or most confusing part of

_____ .

Journals can be easily individualized. Students who benefit from the use of clusters and mind maps might use the left pages for that and the right pages for writing. Students who learn or remember with pictures and symbols can incorporate visuals in their journal. Quotes from the text might be written on one side of a page, and the student's response to the quotes on the other. Journal writing is private, although it may be shared with classmates and will be shared with the teacher. Nevertheless, it is a student's personal record of growth, progress, learning, and individual revelations about personal learning styles and successes.

Journal Topics

You will find Journal Topics on pages:

27, 63, 71

You will find Journal Topics scattered throughout the activities section of this book. For quick reference, see the Journal Topics chart at left.

A check, check minus or check plus may be used to check for the quality of writing. If you don't have the time to read all journals, use a plus or minus in your grade book to indicate whether or not a student has completed each journal assignment. To keep up with journals on a daily basis, I suggest that in each period you collect,

read and respond to three journals In ten days, (two weeks) you will have read thirty students' journals. Read only the journal entry from the day you collect the journal, but do a quick flip-through to be sure the student is writing all the assignments. Reading and responding to three journal entries a day should take no more than five minutes. Journals can be returned to the students or to a storage area immediately.

To respond to a journal entry, simply read it and write a quick response. The teacher is rather like a pen pal, exchanging ideas informally with the writer. What sort of response do you make to a journal entry? Ask a question designed to make the student dig deeper. Give a helpful comment that might clear up a problem. Give praise for good thinking. Focus on the academic subject under consideration. One good question or comment is enough. What your response really does is tell the student that his or her learning process is important to you, that you consider it worth recording and reflecting upon, and that the student is a major participant in his or her own learning.

Writing Portfolio

Have students keep their writing activities from this book in a three ring binder. This collection of writing activities serves as a writing portfolio. Students need to know that writing they do will be

Virginia DeBolt: *Write! Mathematics*
Kagan Cooperative Learning • 1 (800) WEE CO-OP

7

graded somehow, even if it's just for completeness, and that you have a serious commitment to that part of your curriculum. You can grade the material in the binder periodically, perhaps every six weeks.

A more differentiated approach to grading portfolios may include developing a workable grading matrix based on requirements such as completeness, organization, appearance, or other criteria you consider important. You may ask students to provide a table of contents, index, tabs and other helpful aids in their binder. The writing portfolio becomes a record of what the students have learned as well as how students' writing has developed over time. In addition to using the portfolio for grading, have students use it as a tool for reflection about their progress in writing and learning in math.

Using the Writing Activities

In this book you'll find a variety of types of writing activities such as: Writing that enables the student to reflect on his or her thinking; writing that enables the student to remember, clarify, and connect new learning to previous knowledge; writing that augments classroom discussions and activities; writing that lets the teacher see into the student's thought processes; and writing that demonstrates learning to a specified audience.

Many of the writing activities in this book are general, and intentionally so. Because curriculum varies from grade-to-grade and class-to-class, these activities were designed as close to "one size fits all" as possible.

For specific content applications of the activity, see the Idea Bank in each activity for a number of ideas. There is also space under More Ideas for My Class for you to fill in ideas to use the activity with your own curriculum. As you read the activity, make sure to fill in additional ideas. That way, when you begin a topic or unit you can flip through the activities to find the ones that will apply.

Many of the activities can be used meaningfully more than once with new content. Some you may find yourself returning to time and time again.

Between the activities, the journal topics, the Ideas for My Class, and your own writing ideas, you should have more than enough writing topics and activities to integrate writing into your math curriculum all year long.

The writing activities you'll find in this book were designed to incorporate three progressive movements in education: cooperative learning, multiple intelligences, and higher-level thinking. Let's take a quick look at each innovation and how each are included in these activities. We will briefly examine Spencer Kagan's

8

Virginia DeBolt: *Write! Mathematics*
Kagan Cooperative Learning • 1 (800) WEE CO-OP

approach to cooperative learning, Howard Gardner's theory of multiple intelligences, and Benjamin Bloom's taxonomy of thinking.

Cooperative Learning

Research has found that cooperative learning promotes higher achievement than competitive and individualistic learning structures across all age levels, subject areas, and almost all tasks. Writing and math are no exceptions!

Cooperative learning is a natural partner of writing. Cooperative work provides a place for students to brainstorm ideas, develop language and vocabulary, get constructive feedback, and share final works.

Small group interaction provides students with a less threatening environment in which to share their writing and gives every student an equal opportunity to be an active participant throughout the stages of the writing process. An at-risk student, who may have given up on class participation in a whole class structure, is "hooked in" to small group processes and becomes a contributor rather than a distracter.

Cooperative groups supply the teacher with a positive method of channeling the energy to socialize and interact into productive work.

The activities in this book focus on Dr. Spencer Kagan's approach to cooperative learning. For more details on the theory, research and application of cooperative learning, see Dr. Kagan's popular and comprehensive book, *Cooperative Learning*, available from Kagan Cooperative Learning.

In his book, Dr. Kagan outlines six key concepts helpful for making cooperative learning a success in the class. (See box at left). Many of these key concepts are integrated into the activities in this book, especially the cooperative learning structures. The activities in this book work well as stand-alone cooperative events, but work even better in a cooperative classroom environment. Kagan's six keys to cooperative learning are as follows:

1. Teams

A team is a small group of students who work together. For these activities, teams of four are ideal. They are small enough for active participation and split evenly for equal participation during pair work. Teams should be carefully selected by the teacher to reflect a mixture of ability levels, gender and ethnicity. Teams should stay together for approximately six weeks.

2. Will

For cooperative learning to run successfully, students must have the will to cooperate. Classbuilding and teambuilding activities give students the opportunity to

Kagan's 6 Key Concepts

1. **Teams**
2. **Will**
3. **Management**
4. **Skills**
5. **Basic Principles**
6. **Structures**

Virginia DeBolt: *Write! Mathematics*
Kagan Cooperative Learning • 1 (800) WEE CO-OP

9

interact with teammates and classmates in a positive way, promote an environment conducive to successful teamwork, and create a positive class atmosphere. There are three great activity books available from Kagan Cooperative Learning that I can recommend to create the "Will" to cooperate: *Classbuilding, Teambuilding,* and *Communitybuilding.*

3. Management

A number of cooperative management tools helps the teacher run the cooperative classroom more effectively. Kagan describes a host of management tools including using a quiet signal, assigning roles, using modeling, team questions, and more.

4. Skills

Students need social skills such as listening, conflict resolution, and tutoring to work together successfully. Social skills can be taught directly, but with some direction, many can be naturally acquired in the context of cooperative learning.

5. Basic Principles

The are four basic principles to successful cooperative learning summarized by the acronym PIES: **P**ositive Interdependence, **I**ndividual Accountability, **E**qual Participation and **S**imultaneous Interaction. The box at right illustrates the four basic principles and the critical question associated with each principle.

Positive Interdependence
Kagan defines positive interdependence as, "Two individuals are mutually positively interdependent if the gains of either helps the other…Strong Positive Interdependence is created when a student cannot make a gain without a gain of another student. Weak Positive Interdependence is created when a gain for one may produce a gain for another, but it is not *necessary* (italics added)." Students are positively interdependent as they work together to help each other with their writing and learning.

Individual Accountability
Individual Accountability means that each student is responsible for and graded on his or her own learning, contribution, and performance. A student might be held accountable for helping another student learn a new skill in a Pairs Check activity. A student might be held accountable for listening in a Paraphrase activity. A student might be held accountable for learning by passing a test. Most activities have an independent writing component that can be used to hold students accountable for sharing or turning in.

Equal Participation
Equal Participation means that each student has an equal chance to speak, to read, to offer answers and to think. Guarantee Equal Participation by structuring activities so that

PIES
The Principles of Cooperative Learning

Is a gain for one, a gain for another? Is help necessary?

Is individual public performance required?

How equal is the participation?

What percent are overtly active at once?

everyone must participate. Assigning roles is one way to accomplish this. If each person has a job to do, each person is participating. Equal Participation can also be created by using turn taking and turn-taking structures. Turn-taking structures include RoundRobin, RoundTable, RallyRobin, RallyTable, Think-Pair-Share, Three-Step Interview and Pairs Check.

Simultaneous Interaction

Simultaneous Interaction gives you and your students the gift of time. Time for students to read their writing aloud. Time for language development during prewriting. Time for students to manage their own revising and editing when necessary.

How does Simultaneous Interaction give you time? Suppose, for example, that the students have written about the most difficult aspect of their last homework assignment. Having each student share with the class for one minute would take over half an hour. Instead, by pairing students to interact simultaneously to read aloud and discuss their writing, everyone in class can share and respond to the homework in a couple of minutes. In addition to the benefit gained from writing about the homework, students have received the further benefit of speaking and being listened to about it. The time effect of Simultaneous Interaction applies to any writing activity from prewriting to publishing.

Incorporating these four principles in your class activities will insure that you have real, successful cooperative learning happening in your room as opposed to simple group work. These principles are "built-into" the cooperative strategies used throughout the activities.

6. Structures

Structures like RoundRobin and Think-Pair-Share are simple cooperative strategies teachers to use to create learning activities. Structures describe how students interact over the content. There are many structures, each designed to reach different educational objectives.

The activities in this book are based on cooperative structures. Many activities include one cooperative structure, and independent writing. Some activities lead students through a number of cooperative strategies. The procedure for using each cooperative structure is described in each activity. The cooperative structure is listed in the Cooperative Learning section of the intro page. A glossary of structures is provided in the back of the book for easy reference.

Multiple Intelligences

The basic premise of multiple intelligences is that people are smart in many ways. Some people

Virginia DeBolt: *Write! Mathematics*
Kagan Cooperative Learning • 1 (800) WEE CO-OP

11

are particularly good with words; some people are good with math and logic; some people are especially talented with art and spatial relations; some people are good with their hands and bodies; some people are good with music and rhythm; some people are in tune with others; some people are in tune with themselves; and some people are in tune with nature.

Howard Gardner, the originator or the theory of multiple intelligences, called each one of these ways of being smart an intelligence. He originally identified seven intelligences and has added the eighth, the Naturalist. Gardner's eight intelligences are as follows (see box at right):

1. **Verbal/Linguistic**
2. **Logical/Mathematical**
3. **Visual/Spatial**
4. **Bodily/Kinesthetic**
5. **Musical/Rhythmic**
6. **Interpersonal**
7. **Intrapersonal**
8. **Naturalist**

The implication of the multiple intelligences theory for the classroom is that since students are so diverse, classroom learning should reflect the range of intelligences. Students should be given opportunities to develop their strengths as well as opportunities to develop their weaknesses. See the box below for activities ideas for the multiple intelligences.

Integrating writing and science takes naturalist and logical/mathematical content and translates it into a verbal/linguistic form. Teachers can more easily reach and teach linguistic learners. But the activities in this book are much more than solitary writing activities. Being cooperative

The 8 Intelligences

Verbal/Linguistic

Logical Mathematical

Visual/Spatial

Bodily/Kinesthetic

Musical/Rhythmic

Interpersonal

Intrapersonal

Naturalist

Activities for the Multiple Intelligences

Here is a brief list of activities to consider to activate the multiple intelligences.

Verbal/Linguistic
essay, journal, debate, storytelling, portfolios

Logical/Mathematical
out-loud problem solving, puzzles, games, outlines, strategizing

Visual/Spatial
pictorials, flow charts, mindmaps, timelines, models, videotapes, art work

Bodily/Kinesthetic
exhibitions, experiments, models, skits, manipulatives, simulations, role play

Musical/Rhythmic
original songs, dances, rhythmical patterning

Interpersonal
peer review, small group critiques, cooperative learning, leadership

Intrapersonal
reflective journals, goal setting, self-directed projects, self-assessment

Naturalist
observations, logs, categorizing, classifying, experiments

activities, students work in groups and also access and develop their interpersonal intelligence. Additionally, students compose songs, diagram sequences, prioritize alternatives, draw pictures and much more. The multiple intelligences are incorporated throughout the activities. Each activity lists the intelligences used in the Multiple Intelligences section of the intro page.

Higher-Level Thinking

Benjamin Bloom classified different types of thinking skills into a taxonomy, commonly known as Bloom's Taxonomy. His taxonomy of thinking skills is hierarchical. It begins with the lower levels of thinking and moves up to higher-level thinking skills. See Bloom's Taxonomy at left. Higher-Level thinking is usually considered thinking skills beyond the knowledge and comprehension levels.

Much emphasis has been placed lately on incorporating higher-level thinking in the subject areas. Writing is a helpful tool in that direction. Writing by its very nature challenges students to move beyond knowledge and comprehension.

Additionally, many of the activities were written with higher-level thinking skills in mind. Throughout the activities, students apply their knowledge to new situations, use their analytical skills as they delve into issues, pull together different information into a coherent written synthesis, and evaluate the merits of alternatives. The section called Levels of Thinking on the intro page of each activity lists the thinking skills included in the activity corresponding to Bloom's Taxonomy.

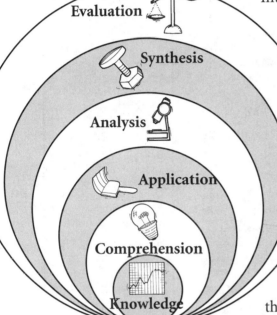

Bloom's Taxonomy

Higher-Level Thinking

↑ 6. Evaluation

5. Synthesis

4. Analysis

3. Application

2. Comprehension

↓ 1. Knowledge

Lower-Level Thinking

In Summary

Integrating writing and math makes math come alive and enriches a student's understanding and appreciation of math! In this book, you will find a treasure chest of cooperative learning, multiple intelligences, higher-level thinking/ writing activities to integrate writing and math!

Virginia DeBolt: *Write! Mathematics*
Kagan Cooperative Learning • 1 (800) WEE CO-OP

13

10 Rules for Writers

1. Write.

2. Write.

3. Write Often.

4. Write about anything.

5. Write about everything.

6. Write about what you see.

7. Write about what you learn.

8. Write about what you think.

9. Write about what you read.

10. WRITE!

Virginia DeBolt: *Write! Mathematics*
Kagan Cooperative Learning • 1 (800) WEE CO-OP

The Writing Process

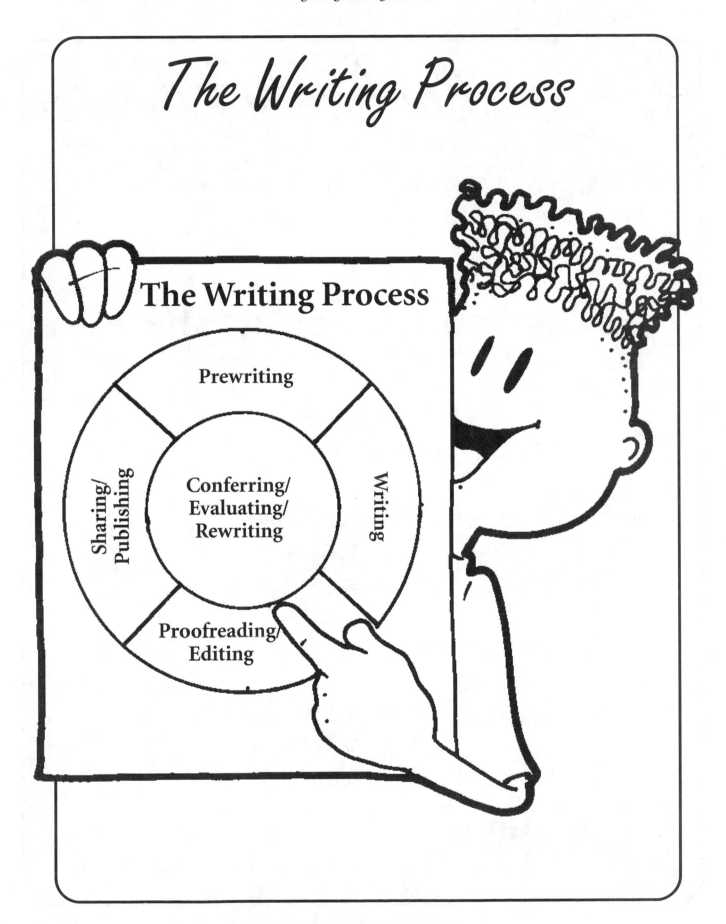

The Writing Process

- Prewriting
- Writing
- Proofreading/Editing
- Sharing/Publishing
- Conferring/Evaluating/Rewriting

Virginia DeBolt: *Write! Mathematics*
Kagan Cooperative Learning • 1 (800) WEE CO-OP

15

Proofreader's Marks

Use these standard marks to show corrections needed in written copy. These symbols are used so that anyone who reads the writing will interpret the corrections in the same way.

⌗
(make a new paragraph)

~~order~~⟝
(take out)

as she
(capitalize)

some one
(close up space)

∧
(add)

by A̸
(make lowercase)

thier
(reverse letters or words)

#
↑
onthe
(insert a space)

soup∧nuts
(add punctuation)

because
~~since~~
(change words)

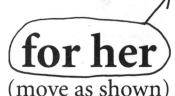
(move as shown)

⊙
(add a period)

Peer Conference Gambit Cards

Directions: Cut out the cards below. Use these sentence starters when you respond to writing.

I like the part where…

I like the way you used the word _____.

What did you mean when you said…

What happened after…

I liked your beginning because…

I would like to know more about…

I had a clear picture in my mind of the part where…

What would you lose if…

What are you going to do next?

Peer Conference Response Form

Author's Name _____

Title _____

Helper's Name _____

Date _____

I like

I want to know more about

One thing you might think about doing

Other

Virginia DeBolt: *Write! Mathematics*
Kagan Cooperative Learning • 1 (800) WEE CO-OP

Peer Response

Title _____

Name _____

_____
_____
_____
_____
_____
_____
_____
_____
_____
_____
_____
_____
_____
_____
_____
_____
_____
_____
_____
_____
_____
_____
_____
_____
_____
_____
_____
_____
_____
_____
_____

Rough Draft

Mathematics Writing Activities

This section of the book consists of thirty-six detailed multiple intelligences cooperative learning, higher-level thinking activities to assist in teaching and writing about math.

The cooperative learning structures used in this section all provide valuable learning experiences, adaptable to any type of content. These structures were selected to lead learners through various stages of thinking and writing about math. I hope your experiences using the structures in these writing activities will open up other ways of applying them in your math curriculum.

For the teacher, there are specific ideas for introducing and using the activities and reproducible blackline masters which can be given to the students.

Interspersed through the activities, you will find Journal Topics pages. Journal topics are brief "just write" activities. They can be used in five or ten minutes at the start or close of Mathematics. The use of journals is explained in more depth on pages 6-7.

Virginia DeBolt: *Write! Mathematics*
Kagan Cooperative Learning • 1 (800) WEE CO-OP

21

List the Steps

Is the class currently learning a new problem solving skill that could be explained in a set of sequential steps? In this activity, students write a description of how to solve the problem. Writing out the sequence of steps helps students verbalize and internalize the steps of solving the problem.

Ideas for my class...	*More ideas for my class...*
List the steps of: • Finding the slope of a line • Measuring an angle • Finding volume • Finding the nearest whole number • Solving an equation • Solving an algorithm • Multiplying fractions • Rounding decimals	• • • • • • • • • • •

I D E A

B A N K

Write-What-I-Do

Group students in pairs. Student A solves a problem, describing the steps of solving the problem aloud. Student B records the steps as Student A describes them. Students switch roles after the first problem is complete so that the student who previously recorded will now work and talk his or her way through the second problem.

Independent Write

Students exchange papers so each student has a record of the steps he or she described. Students write out their steps in paragraph form on the List the Steps reproducible.

Do-What-I-Write

To revise for clarity and completeness, have students exchange their written explanations with a new partner. Students work through a process or problem using their partner's writing. Omissions, unclear or confusing wording, and other communication problems can be identified and changed.

22

Virginia DeBolt: *Write! Mathematics*
Kagan Cooperative Learning • 1 (800) WEE CO-OP

List the Steps

Name _____ Date _____

Directions: Fill in the type of problem in the box below. Use the notes your partner made for you to explain the process or sequence of steps in paragraph form. Make your explanation complete and clear enough so that someone who is not familiar with the problem would be able to solve it using your written explanation.

The steps of _____.
type of problem

Describe the steps in writing _____

_____

_____

_____

_____

_____

_____

_____

_____

_____

_____

_____

_____

_____

_____

Virginia DeBolt: *Write! Mathematics*
Kagan Cooperative Learning • 1 (800) WEE CO-OP

23

Explain What You Know

Having students explain what they know about a topic is useful at the beginning of a new chapter or topic to create interest and focus thinking. It is useful at the end of a chapter to summarize and evaluate what has been learned. In this activity, students brainstorm what they know about the topic, sort and categorize their knowledge, then write what they know.

Cooperative Structures

- 4S Brainstorming
- Team Sort

Level of Thinking

- Comprehension
- Analysis
- Evaluation

Multiple Intelligences

- Verbal/Linguistic
- Logical/Mathematical
- Interpersonal

Ideas for my class...	More ideas for my class...
Explain what you know about:	•
• Integers	•
• Reciprocals	•
• Negative numbers	•
• Prime numbers	•
• Factors	•
• Decimals	•
• Fractions	•
• Multiplication	•

IDEA BANK

4S Brainstorming

Group the students in teams of four for brainstorming. Each student needs several slips of paper. Give each student a role to play in the brainstorming:

- **Speed Captain:** Apply time pressure, push for speed. Research shows that creativity increases with time pressure.
- **Sergeant Support:** Encourage all ideas. Research shows that fluency increases when every contribution is praised during the brainstorming session.

- **Sultan of Silly:** Encourage silly, off-the-wall thinking. It improves creativity and may lead to an idea that works.
- **Synergy Guru:** Encourage piggybacking of ideas.

Announce the topic that the students will explain. For example, "What do you know about negative numbers?" Then, have students brainstorm what they know using the following steps:

1. Student One writes one thing he or she knows about the topic on a card, says it aloud, and places it in the center of the table or desks.

Virginia DeBolt: *Write! Mathematics*
Kagan Cooperative Learning • 1 (800) WEE CO-OP

2. Student Two repeats the process.

3. Each student continues in turn until all the papers are used.

Team Sort

Tell each group of students to sort their dozen or so bits of information into categories. Ask Student Three in each group to record category names and place them above the sorted information. Ask Student Four to check each group member for agreement and understanding of the categories.

Independent Write

On the Explain What You Know reproducible, students use the ideas and categories their group generated to compose several paragraphs about the topic under study. Point out that one way to explain the math concept assigned would be to use each category as the basis for a paragraph in the written work. Ask for other possible ways to organize the writing. Possible answers may include sequentially or according to a mathematical pattern.

Speed Captain

Sergeant Support

Sultan of Silly

Synergy Guru

Virginia DeBolt: *Write! Mathematics*
Kagan Cooperative Learning • 1 (800) WEE CO-OP

25

Explain What You Know

Name _____ **Date** _____

Directions: Fill in the topic in the box below. Write what you know about the topic.

Explain what you know about _____.
topic

Write what you know about the topic. _____

_____

_____

_____

_____

_____

_____

_____

_____

_____

_____

_____

_____

_____

_____

_____

_____

_____

_____

Virginia DeBolt: *Write! Mathematics*
Kagan Cooperative Learning • 1 (800) WEE CO-OP

Journal Topics

- Can you solve the problem a different way?

- Is there an easier way to solve this?

- What picture symbolizes today's learning?

- Tell everything you remember about the homework.

- What three questions do you have about today's lesson?

Define It!

How do you define polygon? How about symmetrical? In this activity, students write their own math definitions, share them with teammates, then write a team definition to share with the class. Writing definitions requires critical thinking and exacting word choice.

ACTIVITY 3

at-a-glance

Cooperative Structures

- RoundRobin
- Team Project
- Simultaneous Chalkboard Share
- Team Discussion

Level of Thinking

- Knowledge
- Comprehension

Multiple Intelligences

- Verbal/Linguistic
- Logical/Mathematical
- Visual/Spatial
- Interpersonal

Independent Write

Give the class a math word to define. For example, when studying angles, have students define "Acute." Students write their definition on the reproducible.

RoundRobin

After a few minutes, have students take turns reading their definitions to teammates.

Team Project

Teams discuss what they like about the individual definitions and work together to write a team definition.

Simultaneous Chalkboard Share

One team representative is selected to write the team's definition on a designated area of the chalkboard.

Team Discussion

Teams read other team's definitions and discuss what they like and don't like about each definition. This process is repeated for each word defined. Students take turns recording the team's definition on the chalkboard.

Define It!

Name _____ **Date** _____

Directions: Fill in the vocabulary words in the boxes below. Write a definition for each word. Be as clear and complete as possible. Be prepared to share your definitions with teammates.

Word _____

Definition _____

_____

Word _____

Definition _____

_____

Word _____

Definition _____

_____

Word _____

Definition _____

_____

Virginia DeBolt: *Write! Mathematics*
Kagan Cooperative Learning • 1 (800) WEE CO-OP

29

Diagram a Sequence

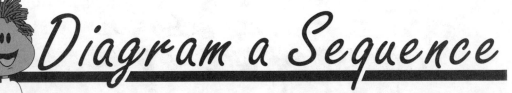

Many mathematical problems can be solved in a sequential series of steps. In this activity, students decide on the steps of solving the problem, create a poster diagraming the sequence, present their posters, then explain the process in writing.

Materials Needed

- Large sheets of paper
- Markers and rulers

Cooperative Structures

- RallyTable
- Team Project
- Teams Present

Level of Thinking

- Analysis
- Synthesis

Multiple Intelligences

- Verbal/Linguistic
- Logical/Mathematical
- Visual/Spatial
- Interpersonal

IDEA BANK

Ideas for my class . . .	More ideas for my class . . .
Diagram the: • Steps of a proof • Steps of an algorithm • Steps of adding unlike fractions • Steps of factoring	• • • • • • • •

RallyTable

Provide the class with a problem that can be solved in a series of sequential steps. For example, the problem can be adding unlike fractions. Pairs work together to list the steps to solve the problem, taking turns writing each step.

Team Project

Two pairs unite as a team of four and compare the steps. They reach consensus on the steps involved, then work as a team to diagram the sequence to solve the problem. The team creates a poster illustrating the steps to solving the problem. Give them a large sheet of paper with which to display a team poster illustrating their set of steps. The team will present their poster to the class.

Teams Present

Teams present their poster to one other team, to various teams, or to the entire class. Each student must participate in the presentation.

Independent Write

Have students write a brief paper explaining the process they have just analyzed and sequenced. The steps in their writing should match the steps as they were displayed on their team's poster.

Virginia DeBolt: *Write! Mathematics*
Kagan Cooperative Learning • 1 (800) WEE CO-OP

30

Diagram a Sequence

Name _____ Date _____

Directions: Fill in the topic in the box below. Write a description of the steps to solve the problem using your team poster.

The steps of _____ .
          topic

Describe the steps in writing. _____

_____

_____

_____

_____

_____

_____

_____

_____

_____

_____

_____

_____

_____

_____

_____

_____

_____

Virginia DeBolt: *Write! Mathematics*
Kagan Cooperative Learning • 1 (800) WEE CO-OP

31

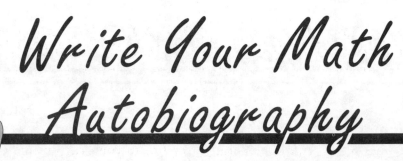
Write Your Math Autobiography

Writing a math autobiography connects students personally to the content. Students reflect on their own math knowledge and come to see themselves as central to the process of learning. In this activity, students create and illustrate math timelines, describe their timelines in writing, then share their math autobiographies with teammates.

ACTIVITY 5

at-a-glance

Cooperative Structure

• RoundRobin

Level of Thinking

• Comprehension
• Analysis
• Application

Multiple Intelligences

• Verbal/Linguistic
• Visual/Spatial
• Logical/Mathematical
• Interpersonal
• Intrapersonal

Ideas for my class . . .	More ideas for my class . . .
• Use this activity to have students write their math autobiographies, feelings about math, anxieties, learning styles, or use of math.	• • • • • • • • •

I D E A **B A N K**

Independent Write

Have students create an illustrated timeline beginning with their earliest math learning and usage on the reproducible. See the sample on page 34-35. The illustrations might provide clues or give indications of *how* the student recalls learning something. This will help them recall their learning and bring feelings about their math successes and failures to the surface. Students then wirte their math autobiography on the reproducible.

RoundRobin

In turn, students share with teammates their illustrated math-timelines and read their written math autobiographies.

Virginia DeBolt: *Write! Mathematics*
Kagan Cooperative Learning • 1 (800) WEE CO-OP

Write Your Math Autobiography

Name _____ **Date** _____

Directions: Create an illustrated timeline of your learning and use of mathematics in the box below. Write your math autobiography. Go back as far as you can remember. Think about what you learned, how and when, about the nature of mathematics and about your ability to do and understand math. What made learning math easy for you? What made it difficult?

Math Timeline

My math autobiography. _____

_____

_____

_____

_____

_____

_____

_____

_____

_____

_____

_____

_____

Virginia DeBolt: *Write! Mathematics*
Kagan Cooperative Learning • 1 (800) WEE CO-OP

33

Write Your Math Autobiography

Sample illustrated math time line
Math Timeline

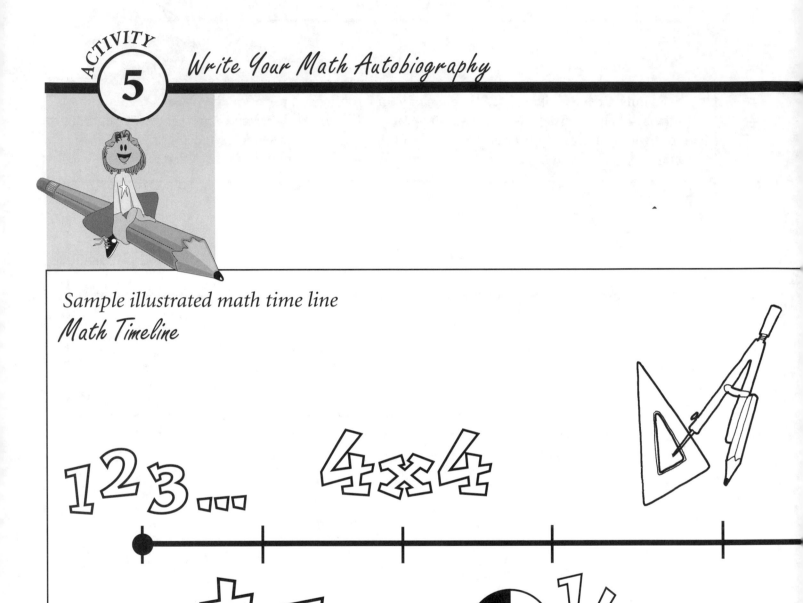

Virginia DeBolt: *Write! Mathematics*
Kagan Cooperative Learning • 1 (800) WEE CO-OP

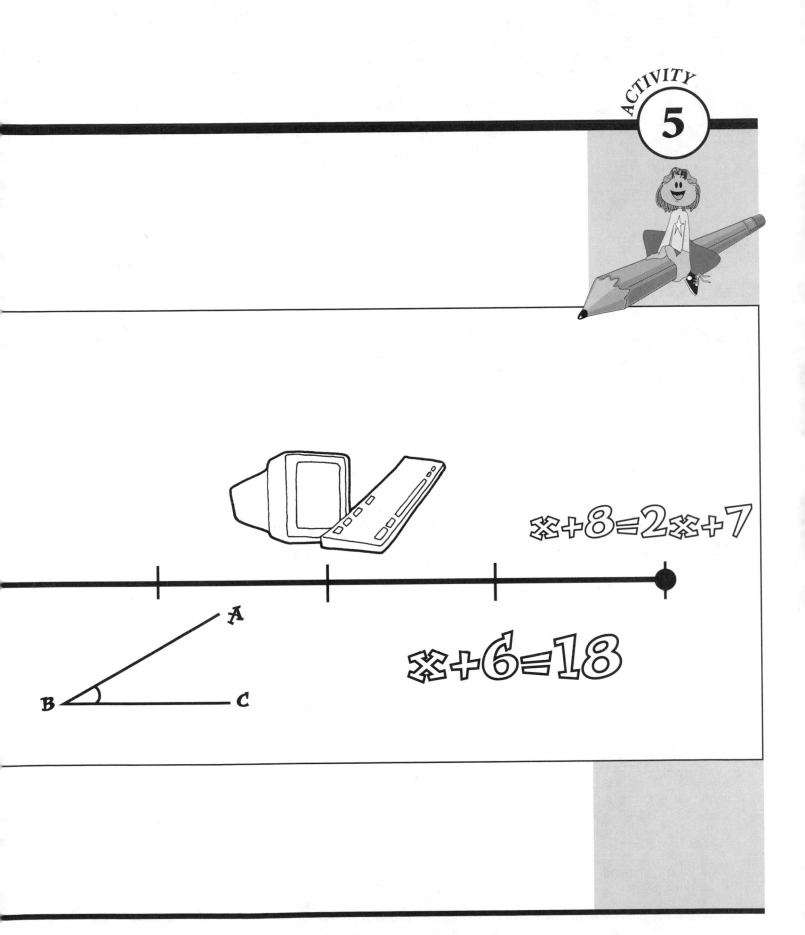

$$x+8=2x+7$$

$$x+6=18$$

Virginia DeBolt: *Write! Mathematics*
Kagan Cooperative Learning • 1 (800) WEE CO-OP

35

Compose Word Problems

Students must think about and communicate math with absolute understanding to compose clear and correct word problems. In this activity, students write and revise word problems, then send them to other teams to solve.

Cooperative Structures

• RoundRobin
• RoundTable
• Send-A-Problem

Level of Thinking

• Synthesis
• Application

Multiple Intelligences

• Verbal/Linguistic
• Logical/Mathematical
• Interpersonal

Ideas for my class...	More ideas for my class...
Compose word problems on:	•
• Problem solving with data	•
• Problems with estimation	•
• Problems with extra data	•
• Problems with percents	•
• Logic problems	•
• Two-step problems	•
	•
	•
	•
	•

IDEA BANK

Independent Write

On the reproducible have students each write three word problems on the math topic you are teaching.

RoundRobin

In a word problem the language and phrasing is crucial. After students have completed their first draft, have them read their three problems to teammates and discuss any needed clarifications or changes.

Independent Write

Students make the necessary corrections to their word problems.

RoundTable

Students read their revised word problems to teammates. When teammates agree on their accuracy and the correctness of the answer, teammates record the word problem on a team word problem sheet and the answer on the reverse side or on an answer key.

Send-A-Problem

When each team has a list of word problems, they send them to other teams to solve.

36

Virginia DeBolt: *Write! Mathematics*
Kagan Cooperative Learning • 1 (800) WEE CO-OP

Compose Word Problems

Name _____ Date _____

Directions: Fill in the topic of word problems in the box below. Write three word problems on the topic and the answers. Share your word problems with teammates.

Word problems on _____ .
topic

Word Problem #1 _____

_____

_____ **Answer**

_____

Word Problem #2 _____

_____

_____ **Answer**

_____

Word Problem #3 _____

_____

_____ **Answer**

_____

Virginia DeBolt: *Write! Mathematics*
Kagan Cooperative Learning • 1 (800) WEE CO-OP

37

Human Model Statistics

We are deluged with numbers and statistics daily. What do these statistics mean? The ability to evaluate and interpret that information gives rise to intelligent decision making. In this activity, pairs discuss how to represent those statistics using their classmates' bodies. Students describe their plans for writing, then a few students are selected to lead the class in forming the human model statistic.

Ideas for my class . . .	More ideas for my class . . .
Use bodies to represent:	•
• Mean, median, mode	•
• Pie charts	•
• Equations	•
• Bar graphs	•
• Probability	•
• Proportion	•
• Ratios	•
• Computing permutations	•
	•
	•

IDEA BANK

Pair Discussion

The class is given a statistic. For example, students may be given the statistic that 3/5 of all cancer deaths are smoking related. Pairs discuss how they could use their classmates to physically represent the statistic For example, they might have the class line up and tell them that they represent 5/5 or 100% of all yearly cancer victims, and have 3/5 of the class slowly expire like wisps of smoke, leaving only 2/5 of the class standing. The fact that the risk of cancer is greatly diminished by choosing not to smoke is made real to the students.

Independent Write

Each student independently writes the directions on the reproducible to have classmates form the human model of statistics

Formations

Select a few students to lead the class in forming a physical model of the statistic.

Virginia DeBolt: *Write! Mathematics*
Kagan Cooperative Learning • 1 (800) WEE CO-OP

Human Model Statistics

Name _____ **Date** _____

Directions: Fill in the statistics that you will describe in the box below. Plan to use your classmates to represent the statistics using their bodies.

My human model for _____

statistics

_____ .

Directions to form the statistics. _____

_____

_____

_____

_____

_____

_____

_____

_____

_____

_____

_____

_____

_____

_____

_____

_____

_____

_____

Virginia DeBolt: *Write! Mathematics*
Kagan Cooperative Learning • 1 (800) WEE CO-OP

39

Design a Brochure

Designing a brochure requires the integration of writing and graphic design skills. In this activity, pairs make a brochure on a math topic, then share their brochures with classmates.

ACTIVITY 8

at-a-glance

Materials Needed

- Sample brochures
- Resources/research materials

Cooperative Structures

- *Pair Project*
- *Pairs Present*

Level of Thinking

- Analysis
- Application
- Synthesis

Multiple Intelligences

- Verbal/Linguistic
- Logical/Mathematical
- Visual/Spatial
- Interpersonal

Ideas for my class...	More ideas for my class...
Design a brochure for: • Life and times of a famous mathematician • Math concept • Math tool like calculators or a compass • Math class	• • • • • • • • • • •

IDEA BANK

Pair Project

Assign the pair a topic for their brochures. All pairs can have the same topic, or each pair can have a different topic. For example, a famous actress will be doing a one-woman show on the life and times of a famous woman mathematician. Create a brochure to be handed out at the performance that will inform the audience about the life and achievements of the mathematician. Pairs research the topic together, and design the brochure together. Students must write part of the brochure copy independently. Have each student write his or her first draft on the Design a Brochure reproducible. Pairs work together to finalize the copy and lay out the brochure. Students may create the brochure on the computer or by hand.

Pairs Present

When pairs have their final brochures, they can share them with another team or can present them to the class.

40

Virginia DeBolt: *Write! Mathematics*
Kagan Cooperative Learning • 1 (800) WEE CO-OP

Design a Brochure

Name_____ **Date** _____

Directions: Fill in the topic of your brochure in the box below. Write your first draft of the copy for your brochure. Work with a partner to finalize your copy and create the brochure.

My brochure on _____.

topic

First draft brochure text. _____

_____

_____

_____

_____

_____

_____

_____

_____

_____

_____

_____

_____

_____

_____

_____

_____

_____

_____

Virginia DeBolt: *Write! Mathematics*
Kagan Cooperative Learning • 1 (800) WEE CO-OP

41

Share Yesterday's Class

Review, anticipatory set, warm-up, getting focused: whatever you call it, five minutes of writing about yesterday's math learning is a great way to start math and to help students build understanding of facts, ideas and vocabulary about the previous day's work. In this activity, students discuss and write about what they learned the prior day.

Cooperative Structure

• Think-Write-Pair-Share

Level of Thinking

• Knowledge
• Comprehension

Multiple Intelligences

• Verbal/Linguistic
• Logical/Mathematical
• Interpersonal

Ideas for my class...	More ideas for my class...
• Use this activity to process and review any prior learning material.	•
	•
	•
	•
	•
	•
	•
	•
	•
	•
	•

IDEA BANK

Think-Write-Pair-Share

Asks students to think about what they did or learned in class yesterday. Students write for five minutes. Pair the students to read their paragraphs to each other.

Allow students to use synergy—those, "Oh, yeah, I forgot about that part," moments —to revise their writing after hearing their partner's work. Select students to share what they've written with the whole class.

42

Virginia DeBolt: *Write! Mathematics*
Kagan Cooperative Learning • 1 (800) WEE CO-OP

Share Yesterday's Class

Name _____ **Date** _____

Directions: Fill in what you learned about in math yesterday in the box below. Describe what you learned in writing. Be prepared to share your writing with a partner and the class.

Yesterday, we learned about _____ .
                                              topic

Describe your learning in writing. _____

_____

_____

_____

_____

_____

_____

_____

_____

_____

_____

_____

_____

_____

_____

_____

_____

_____

Virginia DeBolt: *Write! Mathematics*
Kagan Cooperative Learning • 1 (800) WEE CO-OP

43

Learn from Homework

Use this activity to review, check for understanding, and pinpoint areas of difficulty for students. In this activity, students write about their most difficult homework problem, share their difficulties with teammates, then work together as a team to solve the difficulties.

Ideas for my class...	More ideas for my class...
• Use this activity to check for understanding with any math homework.	• • • • • • • • • • •

I D E A   B A N K

Cooperative Structures

• RoundRobin
• Team Discussion

Level of Thinking

• Comprehension
• Application

Multiple Intelligences

• Verbal/Linguistic
• Logical/Mathematical
• Interpersonal
• Intrapersonal

Independent Write

On the reproducible, have students write about their most difficult homework problem.

RoundRobin

Have each student take turns sharing their most difficult homework problem with teammates.

Team Discussion

The team discusses which particular problem(s) gave them difficulty. Students try to work together to see if they can figure out how to solve the problem. If one student is having difficulties, teammates tutor him or her. If all students are having the same difficulty with the same problem, they write the problem on the board. As a class, review the problems on the board.

Virginia DeBolt: *Write! Mathematics*
Kagan Cooperative Learning • 1 (800) WEE CO-OP

Learn from Homework

Name _____ **Date** _____

Directions: Fill in the problem that gave you the most difficulties in the box below. Write why this problem was the most difficult and what specifically you didn't understand or know how to solve.

My most difficult homework
problem was _____ .
problem

Why was it difficult for you? _____

_____

_____

_____

_____

_____

_____

_____

_____

_____

_____

_____

_____

_____

_____

_____

_____

Elaborate on Alternatives

"I did that another way, but I got the same answer," says the student. "Great," says the teacher. "Can you explain your thinking to us?" The teacher knows that there is more than one mental path through the mathematical mind. In this writing assignment, students develop their mathematical intelligence as they brainstorm alternative routes to solving a problem and assess the relative merits of two alternate routes.

ACTIVITY **11**

at-a-glance

Cooperative Structures

- ThinkPad Brainstorming
- RoundRobin

Level of Thinking

- Evaluation

Multiple Intelligences

- Verbal/Linguistic
- Logical/Mathematical
- Interpersonal

Ideas for my class . . .	More ideas for my class . . .	
• Use this activity to explore and evaluate alternative routes to problem solving, and uncover math "tricks."	• • • • • • • • • •	**I D E A** **B A N K**

ThinkPad Brainstorming

Give students a problem that can be solved in more than one way. Have students brainstorm all the approaches to solving the problem they can think of, writing each solution on a separate scrap of paper.

RoundRobin

After a predetermined amount of time, or after students have a small stack of possible routes to solving the problem, have each student, in turn, share his or her method(s) for solving the problem.

Independent Write

Have students select their favorite two routes, describe them and evaluate their relative merits on the reproducible.

Virginia DeBolt: *Write! Mathematics*
Kagan Cooperative Learning • 1 (800) WEE CO-OP

Elaborate on Alternatives

Name _____ Date _____

Directions: Fill in the problem in the box below. Write a description of the two routes to solve the problem, then decide which method is superior to the other, and cite reasons to justify your reasoning.

Two ways to solve _____ .
                                    the problem

Route #1 _____

_____

_____

_____

_____

_____

_____

_____

Route #2 _____

_____

_____

_____

_____

_____

_____

_____

Which route is better? Why? _____

_____

_____

_____

_____

Profit from Mistakes

Too often, the teaching and learning on a specific math concept is over when the test is given. Students can learn from their mistakes. In this activity, students write down the problems they missed on the test, then roam the room looking for someone who can help them correctly answer the problem.

ACTIVITY

12

at-a-glance

Cooperative Structure

• Find-Someone-Who

Level of Thinking

• Comprehension

Multiple Intelligences

• Verbal/Linguistic
• Logical/Mathematical
• Interpersonal

Ideas for my class . . .	More ideas for my class . . .
• Use this activity to have students tutor each other with any problems they missed on the test or homework	• • • • • • • • • •

I D E A   B A N K

Find-Someone-Who

On the Profit from Mistakes reproducible, students write the problems they missed on the test or homework assignment. Students get out of their seats and try to "Find Someone Who" can help them with a problem they missed. For example, students pair up and Student A asks Student B, "I missed number four. Can you help me figure out what I did wrong?" If Student B knows how to solve the problem, they work through it together. Student A records what he or she did wrong. Student B then asks Student A for help on a problem he or she missed. Student A helps if he or she can. The pair splits up and finds new tutoring partners. Once a student has all his or her problems answered, he or she becomes a helper.

Virginia DeBolt: *Write! Mathematics*
Kagan Cooperative Learning • 1 (800) WEE CO-OP

Profit from Mistakes

Name _____ **Date** _____

Dirctions: Fill in the problems you missed in the box below. Find someone who can help you answer those problems correctly. Work out the problem correctly in the space below and write where you went wrong with each problem you missed.

I missed problems _____.
  problem numbers

Problem _____
Where I went wrong _____
_____

Problem _____
Where I went wrong _____
_____

Problem _____
Where I went wrong _____
_____

Problem _____
Where I went wrong _____
_____

Problem _____
Where I went wrong _____
_____

Virginia DeBolt: *Write! Mathematics*
Kagan Cooperative Learning • 1 (800) WEE CO-OP

49

Job Interviews

Many jobs require high levels of mathematical skills. Have students explore career opportunities and make the connection between math and the real world with this writing activity. In this activity, students interview a person with a math-related career and share their interviews with classmates.

Cooperative Structures

- ThinkPad Brainstorming
- RoundRobin

Level of Thinking

- Comprehension
- Application

Multiple Intelligences

- Verbal/Linguistic
- Logical/Mathematical
- Interpersonal

Ideas for my class . . .	More ideas for my class . . .
Interview people with math-related careers:	•
• Accountant	•
• Banker	•
• Real estate agent	•
• Stock broker	•
• Cashier	•
• Math teacher	•
• Scientist	•
• Engineer	•

I D E A B A N K

ThinkPad Brainstorming

Have students brainstorm interview questions. Students record each question on a thinkpad slip and lay it on the table for teammates to see, to generate more questions.

RoundRobin

After teams have generated a variety of interview questions, have them take turns sharing their questions. Students can record the questions they want to use for their interview on the reproducible.

Independent Write

Students interview a person with a math-related career. They can record the interview or take notes. After the interview, students write it out on a seperate sheet of paper.

RoundRobin

Students take turns reading their interviews and what they learned about the career. The listeners praise the reader when done.

Virginia DeBolt: *Write! Mathematics*
Kagan Cooperative Learning • 1 (800) WEE CO-OP

Job Interviews

Names _____ **Date** _____

Directions: Fill in the career title in the box below. Write six good interview questions to ask your interviewee.

> *My interview with* _____ .
> *career title*

> *Question #1* _____
> _____

> *Question #2* _____
> _____

> *Question #3* _____
> _____

> *Question #4* _____
> _____

> *Question #5* _____
> _____

> *Question #6* _____
> _____

Virginia DeBolt: *Write! Mathematics*
Kagan Cooperative Learning • 1 (800) WEE CO-OP

51

It's Easy If...

Students approach mathematics differently. Some students will create acronyms to remember the steps to solve the problem, some will use their fingers and toes to count, some will draw diagrams, and others will visualize the problem. In this activity, students write about their approach to solving the problem. Students share their techniques with teammates to give others insight into various learning strategies

ACTIVITY 14

at-a-glance

Cooperative Structure

• RoundRobin

Level of Thinking

• Analysis

Multiple Intelligences

• Verbal/Linguistic
• Logical/Mathematical
• Interpersonal
• Intrapersonal

Ideas for my class...	More ideas for my class...
Describe your approach to: • Factoring • Multiplying decimals • Algebra • Square roots • Dividing fractions • Graphing • Fractions	• • • • • • • • • • •

IDEA BANK

Independent Write

Give students the reproducible and specify the topic to be written in the blank. For example, if you are learning about factoring, have students write "*Factoring is easy if…*" Have students write for five to ten minutes, describing their approach to factoring or whatever the topic may be.

RoundRobin

After students have written how to make the topic easy for them, have them take turns reading their work to teammates. After each student reads, the listeners offer one positive comment each, for example, "I thought the way you described how you factor was interesting because it gave me a good idea."

Virginia DeBolt: *Write! Mathematics*
Kagan Cooperative Learning • 1 (800) WEE CO-OP

It's Easy If...

Easy

Name _____ **Date** _____

Directions: Fill in the topic in the box below. Write about what you do to make the topic easy for you.

My approach to _____ .
                              topic

It's easy if _____

_____

_____

_____

_____

_____

_____

_____

_____

_____

_____

_____

_____

_____

_____

_____

_____

Virginia DeBolt: *Write! Mathematics*
Kagan Cooperative Learning • 1 (800) WEE CO-OP

53

How I Feel About It

Students have different feelings about different math topics. Some will love long division and hate graphing. Some will find addition easy and subtraction difficult. It is helpful to have students explore how they feel about the topic and why they feel as they do. In this activity, students share with partners how they feel about the topic, then write a brief reflection on the topic.

Ideas for my class . . .	More ideas for my class . . .
How do you feel about:	•
• Prime numbers	•
• Square roots	•
• Logarithms	•
• Functions	•
• Properties	•
• Rational numbers	•
• Decimals	•
	•
	•
	•

I D E A   B A N K

Think-Pair-Share

Ask students how they feel about a topic. For example, "How do you feel about multiplying decimals?" Give them a good 10-15 seconds of think time, then have them pair and discuss their feelings with a partner on their team. Pick one or two students to share their feelings with the class. Repeat the process, twice more, having students pair with a new partner each time.

Independent Write

Give students the reproducible and let them reflect on their feelings on the topic.

RoundRobin

When done writing, have students take turns sharing their feelings about the topic by reading their reflections to teammates.

Virginia DeBolt: *Write! Mathematics*
Kagan Cooperative Learning • 1 (800) WEE CO-OP

54

How I Feel About It

Name _____ Date _____

Directions: Fill in the topic in the box below. Write how you feel about the topic. Do you like it or not? Does it evoke any emotions? Does it remind you of anything? Why do you think you feel the way you do?

How I feel about _____ .
topic

Describe how you feel about the topic. _____

_____

_____

_____

_____

_____

_____

_____

_____

_____

_____

_____

_____

_____

_____

_____

_____

Virginia DeBolt: *Write! Mathematics*
Kagan Cooperative Learning • 1 (800) WEE CO-OP

55

Be Different!

There are a variety of different ways to represent the same math problem. For example, 2+3=5 could be rewritten as 5=2+3 or as 2+3=6-1 or as a word problem. In this activity, students are each assigned a problem that they rewrite, then present their rewritten problem to teammates. Writing problems differently encourages divergent thinking and stretches mathematical intelligence.

at-a-glance

Cooperative Structure

• Jigsaw

Level of Thinking

• Comprehension
• Application
• Synthesis

Multiple Intelligences

• Verbal/Linguistic
• Logical/Mathematical
• Visual/Spatial
• Interpersonal

Ideas for my class . . .	More ideas for my class . . .
• Equations with decimals	•
• Word problems	•
• Area problems	•
• Adding and subtracting fractions	•
• Percents	•
• Measurements	•
	•
	•

IDEA BANK

Jigsaw

Write four problems on the chalkboard, each with different numbers. A simple addition example: **1)** 5+3=8 **2)** 7+4=11 **3)** 2+6=8 **4)** 9+3=12. Assign each student on a team of four a different problem. Student One gets problem one and so on. Students write their problem on their reproducible. All Student Ones go to a corner of the classroom, Student Twos to another corner and so on. In their corners, students pair up with another student and work to rewrite their problem. Students don't have to come up with the same rewrite, but must agree that their partner's rewrite is accurate. Students then write on their reproducible how they represented the problem differently. Students then reunite with their original teammates and take turns sharing their rewrites and reading their descriptions.

Virginia DeBolt: *Write! Mathematics*
Kagan Cooperative Learning • 1 (800) WEE CO-OP

Be Different!

Name _____ **Date** _____

Directions: Fill in the problem in the box below. Rewrite the problem as differently as you can. Describe how your rewrite is different.

Original problem _____ .

  problem

My rewrite _____ .

Describe how your rewrite is different. _____

_____

_____

_____

_____

_____

_____

_____

_____

_____

_____

_____

_____

_____

_____

Virginia DeBolt: *Write! Mathematics*
Kagan Cooperative Learning • 1 (800) WEE CO-OP

57

Habits of Mind

Help students analyze their own study habits and learn about the study habits of others as well. In this activity, students reflect on and write about their study habits, and share their habits with classmates.

Ideas for my class . . .	More ideas for my class . . .
• Use this activity to have students assess their study habits.	• • • • • • •

I D E A   B A N K

Cooperative Structure

• Think-Write-RoundRobin

Level of Thinking

• Comprehension
• Analysis

Multiple Intelligences

• Verbal/Linguistic
• Logical/Mathematical
• Interpersonal
• Intrapersonal

Think-Write-RoundRobin

Ask students about their study habits. Use the questions on the reproducible. "When do you do your homework?" Give students a little think time, then have them record their answer on the reproducible. Then, give students some time to take turns sharing their answers with teammates.

58

Virginia DeBolt: *Write! Mathematics*
Kagan Cooperative Learning • 1 (800) WEE CO-OP

Habits of Mind

Name _____ **Date** _____

Directions: Answer the following questions about your study habits.

When do you do your homework? _____

_____

_____

Where do you do your homework? _____

_____

_____

Do you do anything else when you do your homework? _____

_____

_____

What do you do if you need help? _____

_____

_____

How do you prepare for a test? _____

_____

_____

What could you do to be more effective with studying? _____

_____

_____

_____

Virginia DeBolt: *Write! Mathematics*
Kagan Cooperative Learning • 1 (800) WEE CO-OP

59

Map Your Mind

A mind map is a visual representation of thoughts. It includes symbols and drawings that map out thoughts and interpretations of ideas. It includes color and graphics, as well as form, to make the information memorable. It gives students a way of recording abstract information in the form of images. In this activity, students create and share their mind maps on the learning material.

IDEA BANK

Ideas for my class . . .	*More ideas for my class . . .*
Create a mind map on:	•
• Estimating sums and differences	•
• Finding least common factor	•
• Determining whether a number is prime or composite	•
• Solve systems of equations using graphs	•
• Explaining place value	•

Independent Write

During or after a presentation on a topic, have students create a mind map on the topic. A mind map is a visual representation of the main idea that integrates color, images, and text. Mind maps are individualized free-form illustrations of one's thinking on the topic. After students complete their mind maps, have them describe it on the back of their papers.

RoundRobin

Students take turns sharing their mind maps with teammates. After each student presents his or her mind maps, teammates can ask questions, clarify confusions or offer praise.

60

Virginia DeBolt: *Write! Mathematics*
Kagan Cooperative Learning • 1 (800) WEE CO-OP

Sample Mind Map

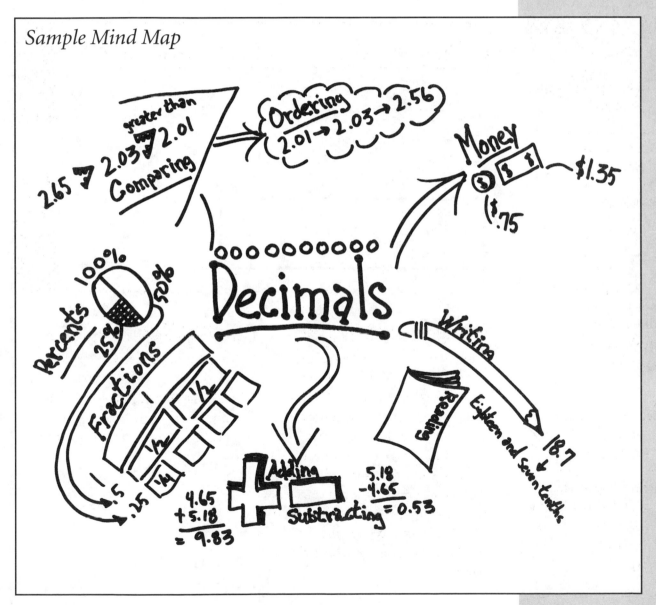

Virginia DeBolt: *Write! Mathematics*
Kagan Cooperative Learning • 1 (800) WEE CO-OP

61

Map Your Mind

Directions: Fill in the topic of your mind map in the box below. Use visuals, symbols, illustrations, arrows, diagrams, writing, color to map out the concept. On the back of this paper, describe your mind map. Be prepared to explain your mind map to another student.

```
_____
            topic
```

Virginia DeBolt: *Write! Mathematics*
Kagan Cooperative Learning • 1 (800) WEE CO-OP

Journal Topics

- What do you want to know about the new chapter?

- Explain how the new chapter is related to the last one.

- What did you learn today?

- Explain spreadsheets.

Virginia DeBolt: *Write! Mathematics*
Kagan Cooperative Learning • 1 (800) WEE CO-OP

63

Perform Your Math

Incorporate the multiple intelligences as you have students perform their math. In this activity each team creates a skit, puppet show, dance, song, pantomime or charade to illustrate a math concept. Students describe their performance, their individual contribution, and assess their own performance.

Cooperative Structures

- Team Project
- Teams Present

Level of Thinking

- Application
- Analysis
- Synthesis

Multiple Intelligences

- Verbal/Linguistic
- Logical/Mathematical
- Visual/Spatial
- Bodily/Kinesthetic
- Musical/Rhythmic
- Interpersonal
- Intrapersonal

Ideas for my class . . .	More ideas for my class . . .
Perform this: • Number patterns • Palindromes • Greatest common divisor • Polygons • Acute & obtuse angles • Multiplying fractions	• • • • • • • • • • •

IDEA BANK

Team Project

Assign each team a different problem relating to the topic. For example, if working on adding fractions, give Team One 3/4+1/2 and Team Two 1/4+1/8. Teammates work together to decide what type of presentation they want to do, teams can do a song, dance skit or puppet show to illustrate the problem. Once they decide on their presentation, students work together to rehearse. Everyone must have a part in the presentation.

Teams Present

Teams can do their math presentation for another team or even for the entire class. This might be a good time to celebrate with cookies and punch, or to invite parents into the classroom to watch the performances.

Independent Write

After all the performances, students each fill out a Perform Your Math reproducible to describe and assess their presentation and their team's performance.

Virginia DeBolt: *Write! Mathematics*
Kagan Cooperative Learning • 1 (800) WEE CO-OP

Perform Your Math

Directions: Fill in the topic of your presentation or math problem in the box below.

Our presentation on _____ .

topic or problem

Describe your presentation: _____

_____

_____

_____

_____

_____

How well did your team do? _____

_____

_____

_____

_____

_____

How well did you do? Cite specifics. _____

_____

_____

_____

_____

_____

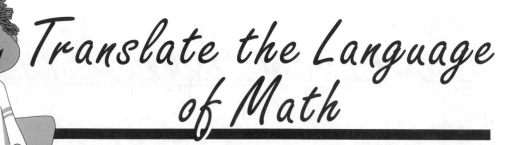

Translate the Language of Math

Math has its own symbolic language. In this activity, each student is assigned a different formula to translate into English and to teach to teammates. If it's true that you never really know something until you teach (explain) it, then this assignment give students an opportunity to really learn about the language of math.

at-a-glance

Cooperative Structure

• Jigsaw

Level of Thinking

• Comprehension
• Application
• Analysis
• Synthesis

Multiple Intelligences

• Verbal/Linguistic
• Logical/Mathematical
• Interpersonal

IDEA BANK

Ideas for my class . . .	More ideas for my class . . .
Translate the formula:	•
• $A = lw$	•
• $A = \pi r^2$	•
• $a^2 + b^2 = c^2$	•
• $y = mx + b$	•
• $V = s^3$	•
	•
	•

Independent Write

Select four formulas for this activity. Assign each student on each team a different formula. Students research their formulas independently then write a first draft version of the formula in plain English on the reproducible.

Jigsaw

Send all students with the same formulas to a corner of the classroom so that in each corner all students are working on the same formula. Students pair up with someone in their corner and share their first draft translations. Then, they work together to write a final draft translation of the formula.

Students return to their original teams to share the final version of the formula with their teammates. The goal for the team is to be sure that each member understands and can give a clear English version of what each formula means.

You may want to use the translations written by the students in matching questions on a future quiz.

Virginia DeBolt: *Write! Mathematics*
Kagan Cooperative Learning • 1 (800) WEE CO-OP

66

Translate the Language of Math

Name _____ Date _____

Directions: Fill in the formula in the box below. Research your formula and write a plain English first draft translation of this formula. Work with a partner to write a final draft of your formula.

My translation of _____ .
formula

First Draft Translation: _____

_____

_____

_____

_____

_____

_____

_____

_____

Final Draft Translation: _____

_____

_____

_____

_____

_____

_____

_____

Virginia DeBolt: *Write! Mathematics*
Kagan Cooperative Learning • 1 (800) WEE CO-OP

67

Real-Life Applications

"Why do I need to learn this? Will I ever use it in real life?" In this activity, teams create a word web of ideas illustrating the real-life applications of the math content. Students then write about three real-life applications and share their writing with teammates.

at-a-glance

Materials Needed

- Crayons or markers
- Large sheets of paper

Cooperative Structures

- Team Word Web
- Teams Present
- RoundRobin

Level of Thinking

- Synthesis
- Analysis

Multiple Intelligences

- Verbal/Linguistic
- Logical/Mathematical
- Visual/Spatial
- Interpersonal

Ideas for my class . . .	More ideas for my class . . .
What are the real-life applications of: • Math • Algebra • Geometry • Trigonometry • Money • Time • Fractions • Decimals	• • • • • • •

IDEA BANK

Team Word Web

Give each team a large sheet of paper and each student a different colored crayon or marker. In the center of the paper, a team recorder writes the topic and puts a box around it. For example, if students are exploring the real-life application of mathematics in general, "Real Life Application of Math" is written in the center box. If instead, students are examining the real-life application of a specific math topic they can write, "Real-life Application of Fractions." Teammates discuss core concepts and when they reach consensus on the core concepts, they write them on the word web with circles around them. When the word web has its basic structure, each student takes their different color crayon or marker and students work simultaneously on the word web adding ideas and details and building bridges between ideas. See the sample word web on the following page.

Teams Present

Teams can share their word webs with another team or with the class.

Independent Write

After sharing and discussing the webs, ask students to write about three real-life applications of the math topic.

RoundRobin

Students take turns reading their writing aloud to teammates. After each student reads aloud, teammates offer the reader a positive comment about his or her applications.

68

Virginia DeBolt: *Write! Mathematics*
Kagan Cooperative Learning • 1 (800) WEE CO-OP

Sample Word Web

Real-Life Application of Math

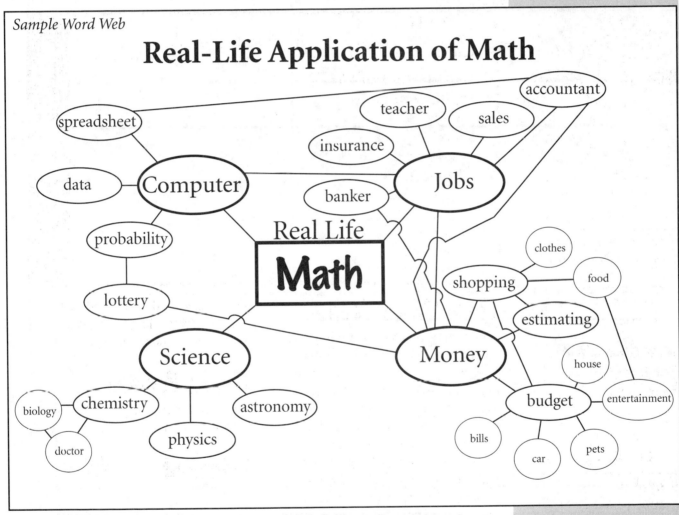

spreadsheet

data

Computer

probability

lottery

Science

biology

chemistry

doctor

physics

astronomy

teacher

insurance

sales

accountant

banker

Jobs

Real Life

Math

clothes

shopping

food

estimating

Money

house

budget

entertainment

bills

car

pets

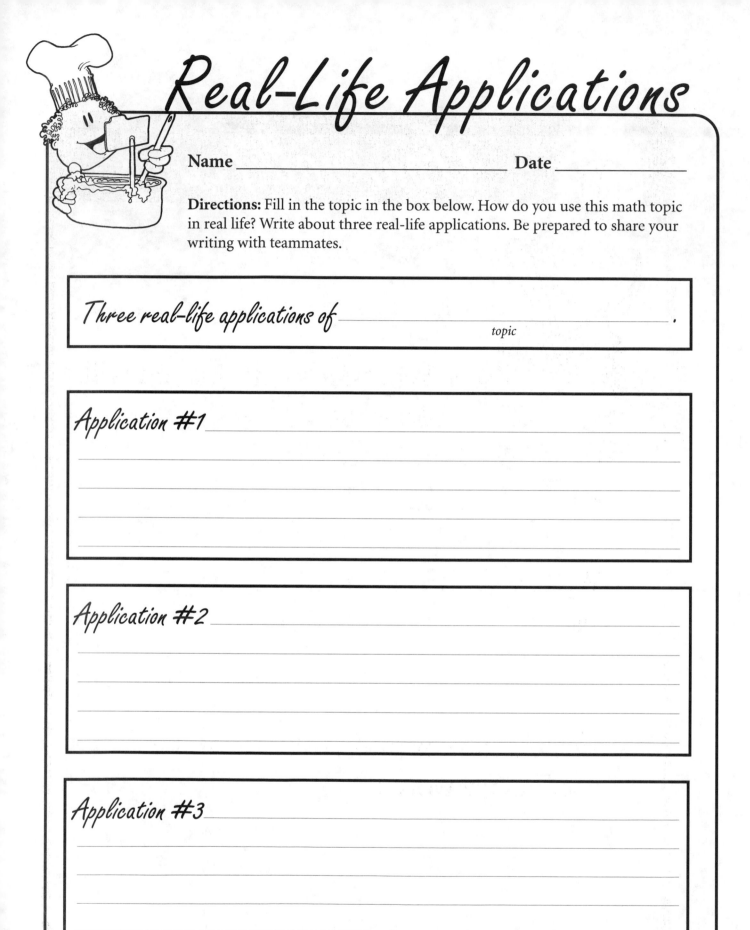

Real-Life Applications

Name _____ **Date** _____

Directions: Fill in the topic in the box below. How do you use this math topic in real life? Write about three real-life applications. Be prepared to share your writing with teammates.

Three real-life applications of _____ .

topic

Application #1 _____

_____

_____

_____

Application #2 _____

_____

_____

_____

Application #3 _____

_____

_____

_____

Virginia DeBolt: *Write! Mathematics*
Kagan Cooperative Learning • 1 (800) WEE CO-OP

Journal Topics

- Discuss Algebra.

- What do you think you will understand after today that you didn't know before?

- Write a six-line poem about today's lesson.

- Write a joke or pun with one of the vocabulary words.

Virginia DeBolt: *Write! Mathematics*
Kagan Cooperative Learning • 1 (800) WEE CO-OP

71

Compare & Contrast

Comparing and contrasting is one of the most fundamental thinking skills. When students compare and contrast in math, they carefully examine the relation of two math topics. In this activity, students analyze two math topics as they compare and contrast them with regard to specific characteristics. Students use this exercise as the basis for a compare and contrast paper.

Cooperative Structure

• Pair Project

Level of Thinking

• Analysis

Multiple Intelligences

• Verbal/Linguistic
• Logical/Mathematical
• Visual/Spatial
• Interpersonal

Ideas for my class...	More ideas for my class...
Compare & Contrast:	•
• Adding/subtracting	•
• Dividing/multiplying	•
• Odd/even numbers	•
• Decimals/fractions	•
• Fractions/percents	•
• Fahrenheit/celsius	•
• Square/rectangle	•
• Acute/obtuse	•
• Concave/convex	•

I D E A   B A N K

Pair Project

The secret of a successful compare and contrast essay is to write about selected features of the two subjects. For example, a student might compare and contrast right triangles and equilateral triangles. A well organized essay would look at the specific features of right triangles and compare and contrast them to the corresponding features of equilateral triangles such as number of angles, degrees of angles, number of sides. (See graphic).

Give students the topics to compare and contrast. Using the Compare & Contrast reproducible, have students work in pairs to come up with how the two objects are similar and how they are different with respect to specific characteristics.

Independent Write

Students can turn their graphic organizer into an interesting paper. Have them begin with an introduction, write a paragraph detailing the likenesses and differences in each of the items compared on the graphic, and finish with a brief summary.

Virginia DeBolt: *Write! Mathematics*
Kagan Cooperative Learning • 1 (800) WEE CO-OP

Compare & Contrast

Name _____ Date _____

Directions: Write the name of the two things you will compare and contrast in the boxes below. Work with a partner to compare and contrast the two items, with regards to three specific characteristics. Write these three characteristics in the arrows below. This sheet will be the basis of your compare and contrast essay.

Write your compare and contrast paper on another sheet.

Virginia DeBolt: *Write! Mathematics*
Kagan Cooperative Learning • 1 (800) WEE CO-OP

73

The World Without Math

A good way to learn to appreciate something we have is to speculate about how life would be if we didn't have it. What would the world be like without math? Without calculators? Without algebra? In this activity, pairs work together to list how the world would be different, then students write their own papers and share them with teammates. This activity helps students see the relevance of various mathematical inventions and concepts, and gives them cognitive practice in cause and effect.

at-a-glance

Cooperative Structures

- RallyTable
- RoundRobin

Level of Thinking

- Analysis
- Evaluation

Multiple Intelligences

- Verbal/Linguistic
- Logical/Mathematical
- Visual/Spatial
- Interpersonal

Ideas for my class...	More ideas for my class...
What would the world be like without:	•
• Math	•
• Place value	•
• Negative numbers	•
• Geometry	•
• Probability theory	•
• Light years	•
• Computers	•
• Zero	•
• The abacus	•

IDEA BANK

RallyTable

In pairs, using the reproducible, students list how the world would be different without the math invention of concept. For example, if the topic was computers, "computers" would be written in the center circle. Students might decide without computers, there would be no internet, with no internet, there may be no E-mail, no online shopping, no net surfing and so on. Students take turns writing the various effects in the graphic organizer.

Independent Write

When pairs have completed their list of effects, each student writes his or her own paper of how the world would be different.

RoundRobin

Students take turns reading their papers to teammates.

74

Virginia DeBolt: *Write! Mathematics*
Kagan Cooperative Learning • 1 (800) WEE CO-OP

The World Without Math

Name _____ **Date** _____

Directions: Fill in the topic in the blank below and in the circle on the left. Work with a partner to list all the ways the world would be different. Then, write your own paper of how the world would be different. Be prepared to share your writing with teammates.

What would the world be like without _____ .
                                              topic

Describe how the world would be different. _____

_____

_____

_____

_____

_____

_____

_____

_____

_____

_____

_____

_____

_____

_____

_____

_____

_____

_____

Virginia DeBolt: *Write! Mathematics*
Kagan Cooperative Learning • 1 (800) WEE CO-OP

75

The Sum of Its Parts

Acrostic poems use every letter of the topic word as the beginning letter for a sentence or phrase about the topic. In this activity, students create acrostic poems on a math topic and share their poems with the class.

at-a-glance

Cooperative Structures

- Think-Write-RoundRobin
- Simultaneous Chalkboard Share

Level of Thinking

- Comprehension
- Application
- Synthesis

Multiple Intelligences

- Verbal/Linguistic
- Logical/Mathematical
- Visual/Spatial
- Bodily/Kinesthetic
- Musical
- Interpersonal

Ideas for my class . . .	More ideas for my class . . .
• **Write acrostic poems with:** • Any word that represents an important math concept • Algebra • Fractions • Decimals • Division • Equation • Geometry	• • • • • • • •

IDEA BANK

Think-Write-RoundRobin

Announce the topic of the acrostic poem and write it on the chalkboard. For example, "Fractions" may be the topic. Have students think of a sentence or phrase describing fractions that begins with the letter "F." Students write their ideas on their reproducible, then share their ideas with teammates. For example, students may come up with, "Four equal parts are called fourths," or Fewer than one whole," or "Find the number of parts," or "Friends and relatives of decimals."

Simultaneous Chalkboard Share

Teammates pick one phrase that captures the essence of the topic. Send Student Ones to the chalkboard to write "Fraction" vertically in the team's designated area and write the first "F" phrase. Have students Think-Write-RoundRobin every letter of the word and take turns recording the team's favorite on the chalkboard. When done, each student will have their own acrostic poem and each team will have their own unique poem on the chalkboard to share with the class.

76

Virginia DeBolt: *Write! Mathematics*
Kagan Cooperative Learning • 1 (800) WEE CO-OP

The Sum of Its Parts

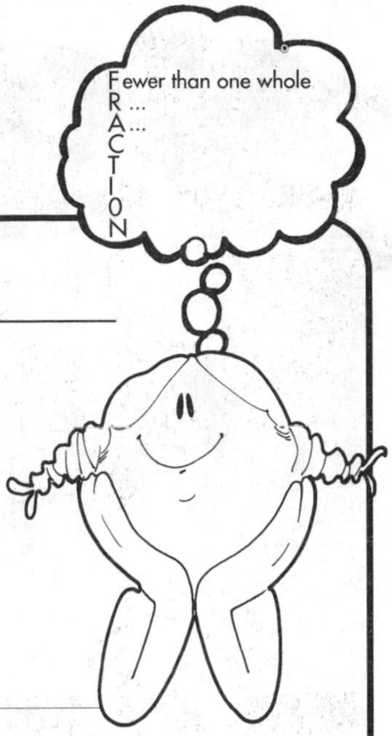

Name _____ **Date** _____

Directions: Fill in each letter of th topic word on its own line, down the left side of the paper. Write a phrase or sentence about the topic beginning with each letter.

letter   *is for*

_____   _____

_____   _____

_____   _____

_____   _____

_____   _____

_____   _____

_____   _____

_____   _____

_____   _____

Math Book Report

The library is loaded with math books. There are math text books, books on teaching math, math literature books and more. Have students explore the rich world of mathematical writing. In this activity, students read or review a math book, write a book report, then share their findings with teammates.

at-a-glance

Cooperative Structure

• RoundRobin

Level of Thinking

• Comprehension
• Application

Multiple Intelligences

• Verbal/Linguistic
• Logical/Mathematical
• Interpersonal

IDEA BANK

Ideas for my class . . .	More ideas for my class . . .
Math books for reports:	•
• *Zero to Lazy Eight.* Alexander Humez, Nicholas Humez & Joseph Maguire	•
• *Innumeracy.* John Allen Paulos	•
• *Pi in the Sky.* John D. Barrow	•
• *The Statistical Pioneers.* James W. Tankard	•
• *Do You Wanna Bet?* Jean Cushman	•
• *Geometry for Every Kid.* Janice Van Cleave	•
• *Math Mini Mysteries.* Sandra Markle	•

Independent Write

Tell the students to read or review a book on a math topic. You might suggest some from the Idea Bank, or tell the students to begin by looking for books with Dewey decimal classification numbers 510, 793, or 001.64. Students can even review their own textbooks. Using the reproducible, students write a book report on their math book.

RoundRobin

Students take turns presenting their book reports to teammates. Each student has three minutes to present. (A few practice sessions at home to work out a three-minute presentation would be helpful.) The teacher keeps time and announces when it is time for the next student on each team to begin. The entire class will have completed an oral book report in approximately 12 minutes.

Virginia DeBolt: *Write! Mathematics*
Kagan Cooperative Learning • 1 (800) WEE CO-OP

Math Book Report

Name _____ **Date** _____

Directions: Write a report about a book on a math topic. Tell what you learned by reading the book. Tell what you liked about the book, and what you didn't like.

Title: _____

Author: _____

Publisher & Copyright date: _____

Summary of book & math topics covered _____

_____

_____

_____

_____

_____

_____

_____

_____

Evaluation of book _____

_____

_____

_____

_____

_____

_____

_____

Virginia DeBolt: *Write! Mathematics*
Kagan Cooperative Learning • 1 (800) WEE CO-OP

79

Math Masterpieces

Many math concepts can be found in art: patterns, symmetry, shapes, spatial relations. Art can also be used to illustrate math concepts. In this activity, students develop their visual/spatial intelligence as they create math art to represent the math concept.

ACTIVITY 26

at-a-glance

Cooperative Structures

- Think-Pair-Share
- RoundRobin

Level of Thinking

- Application

Multiple Intelligences

- Verbal/Linguistic
- Logical/Mathematical
- Visual/Spatial
- Interpersonal

Ideas for my class . . .	More ideas for my class . . .
Create math artwork:	•
• Tessellation	•
• Shape creation	•
• Graphs	•
• Illustrate money	•
• Symmetrical prints	•
• Pattern design	•
• Scale drawings	•

IDEA BANK

Think-Pair-Share

Ask the class how they could make artwork to represent the math learning topic. For example, when learning about patterns, ask the class, "What kind of artwork could you create to illustrate the concept of patterning?" Have students think for 10-15 seconds, then pair up to share their ideas. Select a few students to share their ideas with the class. Some ideas might include: "You can design a quilt that has a repeating pattern," or, "You can make a border out of repeating geometric shapes."

Independent Write

Have students work independently to make a math masterpiece on the reproducible, illustrating the concept, then describe it in writing.

RoundRobin

Students take turns reading their descriptions of their math masterpieces and sharing their illustrations with teammates. The math masterpieces can be posted in the class to share with classmates.

Virginia DeBolt: *Write! Mathematics*
Kagan Cooperative Learning • 1 (800) WEE CO-OP

Math Masterpieces

Name _____ **Date** _____

Directions: Illustrate the math concept in the box below. Write a description of how your illustration uses the math concept.

Illustration

Describe your masterpiece _____

_____

_____

_____

_____

_____

_____

_____

_____

_____

_____

Virginia DeBolt: *Write! Mathematics*
Kagan Cooperative Learning • 1 (800) WEE CO-OP

81

Classify Your Numbers

We use numbers as symbols to represent a wide range of things like temperature (80°F), time (12:48pm), percents (40%), degrees (45°), fractions (3/8). In this activity, teams brainstorm various types of numbers. Students work together to classify the numbers, then independently write about their number classification system.

ACTIVITY 27

at-a-glance

Cooperative Structures

- ThinkPad Brainstorming
- Teams Sort
- Teams Present
- Pair Project

Level of Thinking

- Analysis

Multiple Intelligences

- Verbal/Linguistic
- Logical/Mathematical
- Visual/Spatial
- Interpersonal

Ideas for my class . . .	More ideas for my class . . .
Classify these numbers:	•
• Sets of fractions, decimals & percents	•
• Sets of numbers in patterns	•
• Sets of multiples	•
• Sets of factors	•
• Unrelated numbers	•

ThinkPad Brainstorming

In teams of four, every student has a pen and a number of thinkpad slips. Have students brainstorm as many different types of numbers as they can, writing each one on a thinkpad slip, then placing it face up on the desk for teammates to see. When done, students have a pile of numbers which they will sort.

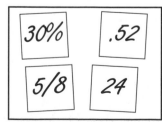

Team Sort

Students work together as a team to make a classification for the numbers that they generated. The classification system must accommodate all the numbers. Show students the Sample Graphic Organizers on page 85 for classification ideas. The categories can be written on a large sheet of paper. Students take turns placing their numbers in the categories.

82

Virginia DeBolt: *Write! Mathematics*
Kagan Cooperative Learning • 1 (800) WEE CO-OP

Teams Present

When done with their number systems, teams can share their method of classification with another team or with the class. To share with another team, have Team A visit Team B. Team B describes their system. To share with the class, have students tape their thinkpad slips to the paper and post it in front of the class for teams to see.

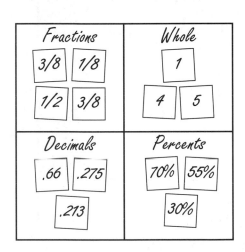

Pair Project

Pairs work to rewrite their classification system as an outline on the reproducible.

I. Fractions
   A. 3/8
   B. 1/2
   C. 1/8
   D. 1/4

II. Decimals

Independent Write

The movement from graphic organizer to outline to paragraph is a natural one. Have students write paragraphs explaining their classification systems on the reproducible.

Virginia DeBolt: *Write! Mathematics*
Kagan Cooperative Learning • 1 (800) WEE CO-OP

83

Classify Your Numbers

Name _____ **Date** _____

Directions: Work with a partner to create an outline of your number classification system. Then, use your outline to write your own description of your classification of the numbers.

Outline

Description _____

_____

_____

_____

_____

_____

_____

_____

_____

_____

_____

_____

_____

_____

_____

_____

_____

_____

_____

_____

_____

_____

Virginia DeBolt: *Write! Mathematics*
Kagan Cooperative Learning • 1 (800) WEE CO-OP

Sample Graphic Organizers

The Ladder

Venn Diagram

The Spider Web

The Continuum

The Tree

The Chain

The Matrix

The Mind Map

Virginia DeBolt: *Write! Mathematics*
Kagan Cooperative Learning • 1 (800) WEE CO-OP

85

Measuring the Untouchable

Some things are not easily measured. How do you measure the height of a building, flagpole, or crater on the moon? In this activity, students write a plan to measure the untouchable and share their plans with teammates.

ACTIVITY

28

at-a-glance

Cooperative Structure

• RoundRobin

Level of Thinking

• Application

Multiple Intelligences

• Verbal/Linguistic
• Logical/Mathematical
• Visual/Spatial
• Bodily/Kinesthetic
• Interpersonal

Ideas for my class...	*More ideas for my class...*
How do you measure:	•
• Surface area of school outside walls	•
• Height of flagpole	•
• Surface area of classroom ceiling	•
• Height of a tree in school yard	•
• Height of a nearby tall building or church steeple	•
• Height of goal post	•

I D E A  **B A N K**

Independent Write

Assign the class a measuring task that involves skills they are learning about. For example, if learning about surface area, have students devise a plan to measure the surface area of the school's exterior walls. Students write their plan on the reproducible.

RoundRobin

Students get in their teams and take turns reading their plan to teammates. After each teammate shares, the listening teammates offer ideas to help clarify the plan.

Independent Write

Students can revise their first drafts if necessary.

Extension activity

Have teammates switch plans and try to measure the object using the instructions provided. Students can work with the writer to revise the instructions to make them more helpful.

Virginia DeBolt: *Write! Mathematics*
Kagan Cooperative Learning • 1 (800) WEE CO-OP

Measuring the Untouchable

Name _____ **Date** _____

Directions: How would you measure something you were unable to physically touch? For example, how do you measure the size of a crater on the moon, the distance to the top of a tall building, or the height of a breaking wave? How would you verify your measurement? Explain your plan to measure the assigned object. Be prepared to share your plan.

My plan to measure _____ .

                                                       object

Describe your plan. _____

_____

_____

_____

_____

_____

_____

_____

_____

_____

_____

_____

_____

_____

_____

_____

_____

_____

Virginia DeBolt: *Write! Mathematics*
Kagan Cooperative Learning • 1 (800) WEE CO-OP

87

The Rhythm of Math

Music, song and poetry are rhythmic. Rhythms can be thought of as repeated patterns. Much of math involves rhythmic patterns too. In this activity, students work to create a song or poem about a math topic, then present it to another pair or to the class.

ACTIVITY 29

at-a-glance

Cooperative Structures

• Pair Project
• Pairs Present

Level of Thinking

• Synthesis

Multiple Intelligences

• Verbal/Linguistic
• Logical/Mathematical
• Interpersonal
• Musical/Rhythmic

Ideas for my class . . .	More ideas for my class . . .
Create a song or poem about: • A definition • A set of steps • A process • A formula • A proof • Number families • Mathematics • Mathematician	• • • • • • • • • • •

IDEA BANK

Pair Project

Assign pairs a topic about which to create a poem or song. The song can be about any mathematical topic, about a mathematician, how to solve a problem or even about math in general. Partners work together to write the lyrics to their song or poem. Some research may be involved. Partners then plan how they are going to present their poem or song. They may sing it as a duet, read some parts in unison and some independently, or may even add sounds. One easy method is to create a song to a well-known melody like Twinkle Twinkle Little Star or Jingle Bells.

Pairs Present

Pairs share their mathematical song or poems with another pair or with classmates.

Virginia DeBolt: *Write! Mathematics*
Kagan Cooperative Learning • 1 (800) WEE CO-OP

The Rhythm of Math

Names _____ **Date** _____

_____

Directions: Fill in the topic of your song or poem in the box below. Be prepared to share your song or poem with classmates.

Our song/poem about _____ .

topic

Write your song lyrics. _____

_____

_____

_____

_____

_____

_____

_____

_____

_____

_____

_____

_____

_____

_____

_____

_____

Virginia DeBolt: *Write! Mathematics*
Kagan Cooperative Learning • 1 (800) WEE CO-OP

89

Math Jeopardy!

Jeopardy is a quiz show in which the answer is presented and contestants try to provide the correct question. Use this fun variation to play Jeopardy in teams. In this activity, teams create questions and answers about the topic. They send the answers to another team to provide the questions.

Cooperative Structures

• RoundRobin
• Send-A-Problem

Level of Thinking

• Analysis

Multiple Intelligences

• Verbal/Linguistic
• Logical/Mathematical
• Interpersonal

Ideas for my class . . .	More ideas for my class . . .
• Play Math Jeopardy with any math content for practice or review.	• • • • • • • • •

I D E A

B A N K

Independent Write

Have students work independently to write answers and questions about the topic you want to review. For example, when learning about calculating area, the answer may be, "Multiply the length times the width." The question is, "How do you find the area of a rectangle?" Instruct students not to create answers like "2" where any range of questions may be correct.

RoundRobin

Students share their questions and answers with teammates.

Send-A-Problem

Teammates select their best questions and answers and write the answers on a sheet of paper with the questions on the reverse side or on an answer key. Answers can also be written on index cards with the questions on the back. When each team has a set of questions and answers, they send them to another team to play Jeopardy. Teammates take turns reading the answer. The first teammate to provide the questions receives points.

Virginia DeBolt: *Write! Mathematics*
Kagan Cooperative Learning • 1 (800) WEE CO-OP

Math Jeopardy!

Name _____ **Date** _____

Directions: Fill in the Jeopardy math topic in the box below. Write review questions and answers. Make sure the answers only have one correct question.

Jeopardy questions and answers on _____ .
topic

Q _____

A _____

Q _____

A _____

Q _____

A _____

Q _____

A _____

Q _____

A _____

Virginia DeBolt: *Write! Mathematics*
Kagan Cooperative Learning • 1 (800) WEE CO-OP

91

Personalize Your Math

Mathematics has its own language. With the unfamiliar jargon it can be foreign to students. Make the language of math more personally relevant for your students. In this activity, students write personally relevant sentences with math vocabulary words. Students share their sentences with teammates.

ACTIVITY 31

at-a-glance

Cooperative Structure

• RoundRobin

Level of Thinking

• Application

Multiple Intelligences

• Verbal/Linguistic
• Logical/Mathematical
• Interpersonal
• Intrapersonal

Ideas for my class...	More ideas for my class...
• Use this activity to write sentences with any math vocabulary words.	• • • • • • •

IDEA BANK

Independent Write

On the reproducible, students fill in a math vocabulary word, then use the math vocabulary word in a sentence that demonstrates an understanding of the word. The sentence must also be about the author. For example, a sentence using the word "asymmetrical" might be: This morning, I looked somewhat *asymmetrical* because I was in such a hurry that I wore one black and one blue sock to school.

RoundRobin

Students take turns reading their sentence to teammates. Teammates must listen carefully to make sure the word is used properly in the sentence. Teammates work together to rewrite any unclear sentences.

Virginia DeBolt: *Write! Mathematics*
Kagan Cooperative Learning • 1 (800) WEE CO-OP

Personalize Your Math

Name _____ **Date** _____

Directions: Fill in the math vocabulary words in the boxes below. Write a sentence that shows correct use of the vocabulary in a way that cleverly demonstrates the meaning of the word. You must include yourself in the sentence.

Word _____
Sentence _____
_____

Word _____
Sentence _____
_____

Word _____
Sentence _____
_____

Word _____
Sentence _____
_____

Word _____
Sentence _____
_____

Virginia DeBolt: *Write! Mathematics*
Kagan Cooperative Learning • 1 (800) WEE CO-OP

93

Personal Problems

Word problems are a natural mix of writing and mathematics. In this activity, students write personally relevant word problems, and share them with teammates. Then, teams write a team word problem and share it with other teams.

ACTIVITY 32

at-a-glance

Cooperative Structures

• RoundRobin
• Team Project
• Simultaneous Chalkboard Share

Level of Thinking

• Application
• Synthesis

Multiple Intelligences

• Verbal/Linguistic
• Logical/Mathematical
• Interpersonal
• Intrapersonal

Independent Write

Write four problems on the board relating to the topic of study. A simple algebra example: 1) 2x=4, 2) 3x=6, 3) 4x=12, 4) 4x=8. Student One writes a word problem about the problem one, Student Two about problem two and so on. One rule: the student must be the topic of his or her own word problem.

RoundRobin

Teammates take turns sharing their personal word problems.

Team Project

Write a more challenging problem on the board. For example: 3x+4=13. Have teams work together to write a word problem about the problem. One rule: All teammembers' names must be included in the word problem.

Simultaneous Chalkboard Share

One student from each team writes the team's word problem on a designated area of the chalkboard to share with other teams.

Independent Write

Write one more challenging problem on the chalkboard. Have students write a word problem about the problem on the reproducible. Again, students must be the subjects of their word problems

Personal Problems

Name _____ **Date** _____

Directions: Fill in your assigned problem in the box below. Write a word problem about the problem. Include yourself in your word problem. See how creative you can be.

Write a personal word problem for: _____ .
topic

Word problem _____

_____

_____

_____

_____

_____

_____

_____

_____

_____

_____

_____

_____

_____

_____

_____

_____

_____

_____

Virginia DeBolt: Write! Mathematics
Kagan Cooperative Learning • 1 (800) WEE CO-OP

95

Build Your Math

Numbers are symbolic representations of concrete things, used to calculate and quantify. Bring that abstraction back to a touchable level with models or dioramas. In this activity, students connect symbols with concrete objects as they build and present their math.

ACTIVITY 33

at-a-glance

Materials Needed

• Objects or manipulatives to build math problems

Cooperative Structures

• Team Project
• Teams Present

Level of Thinking

• Application
• Analysis
• Synthesis

Multiple Intelligences

• Verbal/Linguistic
• Logical/Mathematical
• Visual/Spatial
• Bodily/Kinesthetic
• Interpersonal

Ideas for my class...	More ideas for my class...
Build the following:	•
• Pie and bar graphs	•
• 3/4+1/2= 1 1/4	•
• 3x8=24	•
• 12÷4=3	•
• (0,1)(1,1)(2,2)(3,3)	•
• Frequency distribution	•
• 10% off of $65	•
	•
	•

IDEA BANK

Team Project

Assign each team in the class a variation of the same type of problem. For example, if studying adding decimals, assign Team One 5.13 +8.25, Team Two 6.23 + 7.41 and so on. Have students work together to build their math problems using physical objects or math manipulatives. Some objects and manipulatives to build problems or concepts include: Base 10 materials, fraction manipulatives, buttons, blocks, cubes, pattern blocks, legos. For this example, student may build their decimal problems with base 10 manipulatives on a place value mat. Teammates make sure everyone on the team under-stands how the concrete manipulatives represent the number symbols as everyone must take part in the presentation and write their own description.

Teams Present

Teams present their math constructions to another team or may even present it to the class. Teammates plan who is to present what. Every teammember must have a role in the presentation.

Independent Write

After the presentations, students write on the reproducible how numbers symbolize concrete operations.

Virginia DeBolt: *Write! Mathematics*
Kagan Cooperative Learning • 1 (800) WEE CO-OP

Build Your Math

Name _____ **Date** _____

Directions: Fill in the math problem or concept you built with teammates. Describe how you built it and how numbers are used to symbolize a concrete operation.

We built _____ .

math problem or concept

How do numbers symbolize the concrete operation? _____

_____

_____

_____

_____

_____

_____

_____

_____

_____

_____

_____

_____

_____

_____

_____

_____

Explain the Need

Why, why, why? Why do we need math? Why do we need to learn base two? Why do we need integers? Sound familiar? In this activity, students explore the need for learning about mathematics.

Cooperative Structures

• Simultaneous RoundTable
• RoundRobin

Level of Thinking

• Synthesis

Multiple Intelligences

• Verbal/Linguistic
• Logical/Mathematical
• Interpersonal

Ideas for my class . . .	More ideas for my class . . .
Explain why we need:	•
• Zero	•
• Place value	•
• Powers	•
• Expanded notation	•
• Graphs	•
• Least common multiples	•
• Ratios	•
• Histograms	•
• Odds	•
	•
	•

I D E A   B A N K

Simultaneous RoundTable

Each student pulls out a sheet of paper and writes on the top, "Why do we need _____?" the topic should be general enough so that students can come up with many reasons why we need it. For example, "Why do we need graphs?" To be more specific, assign each student on the team a different related topic. For example, Student Ones: line graphs, Student Twos: bar graphs, Student Threes: pie graphs, Student Fours: frequency distribution. Students write down one idea why we need the topic,

then pass the paper clockwise for a teammate to make the next contribution. In a team of four, four papers are simultaneously being passed around the team.

RoundRobin

After a determined amount of time or when students have a list of ideas, have them take turns reading the ideas on their sheet to teammates.

Independent Write

Students use the ideas they came up with to write why we need the math topic or concept they learned about or will learn about.

98

Virginia DeBolt: Write! Mathematics
Kagan Cooperative Learning • 1 (800) WEE CO-OP

Explain the Need

Why?

Name _____ **Date** _____

Directions: Fill in the math topic or concept in the box below. Write why we need this math topic or concept. Use some of the ideas you came up with your team.

Why do we need _____ ?

topic

Describe why we need this math topic. _____

_____

_____

_____

_____

_____

_____

_____

_____

_____

_____

_____

_____

_____

_____

_____

_____

_____

_____

Virginia DeBolt: *Write! Mathematics*
Kagan Cooperative Learning • 1 (800) WEE CO-OP

99

Teach Texts

Wouldn't it be fun for students to present their own math books to younger students? In this activity, pairs write a book for younger students then share their math books with younger students.

ACTIVITY 35

at-a-glance

IDEA BANK

Ideas for my class...	More ideas for my class...
Create a book on: • ABC books using math words • Counting books • Geometric shapes books • Sports math books • Measurement books	• • • • • • • • • • •

Pair Project

Get together with a teacher who teaches math to younger students. If he or she would like your students to share their math books with his or her class, decide on the topic of the books. Then assign pairs of students to work together to create the book on the topic. The project may take several days to complete. Pairs begin by writing a rough draft of their book. You may want them to hand in the rough draft for your approval before they begin the actual book. Then the pairs work to complete the book by the due date. Students can create their books by hand, but encourage them to use the computer if possible. Have each pair use the information in the reproducible as a guide.

Pairs Present

Pairs present their books to small groups of students in the other class. They can do several rounds of sharing, each time with a new audience. Pairs can also present their books to other pairs in their own class.

100

Virginia DeBolt: *Write! Mathematics*
Kagan Cooperative Learning • 1 (800) WEE CO-OP

Teach Texts

Names _____ **Date** _____

_____ **Due Date** _____

Directions: Work with a partner to write a book about math for younger students. Use this checklist to help you as you write and create your book.

_____ Select a type of book. (Pop-up book, picture book, story book...)

_____ Write a rough draft. Contribute equally to the writing or divide the writing work.

_____ Decide on a title. _____

_____ Decide on the size of the book. _____

_____ Decide on the type of cover to make. _____

_____ Decide on the type of binding to use. _____

_____ Lay out a practice book and decide what will appear on each page.

_____ Write and illustrate each page including the cover and a title page.

Virginia DeBolt: *Write! Mathematics*
Kagan Cooperative Learning • 1 (800) WEE CO-OP

101

Evaluate It!

Do you want to know what students find easy, difficult, memorable, boring, effective, ineffective, fun, drudgery? Here's how to find out. In this activity, students make a personal connection with the content as they write about what they like and dislike.

ACTIVITY

36

at-a-glance

Cooperative Structures

• Think-Write-
  RoundRobin
• RoundRobin

Level of Thinking

• Evaluation

Multiple Intelligences

• Verbal/Linguistic
• Logical/Mathematical
• Interpersonal
• Intrapersonal

Ideas for my class...	*More ideas for my class...*
• Use this activity to evaluate any learning materials or even at the end of the quarter, semester or year to evaluate the class.	• • • • • • • • • •

IDEA BANK

Think-Write-RoundRobin

Ask students to reflect on the positive aspects of the learning topic. For example, "What did you like about writing proofs?" Give students some time to think about the prompt, then write some ideas. Then have students share their ideas in turn with teammates. Repeat the process with a question reflecting on the negative aspects of the learning topic, "What did you dislike?"

Independent Write

After sharing their likes and dislikes with teammates, have students evaluate the topic on the reproducible.

RoundRobin

Have students take turns reading their evaluations to teammates.

102

Virginia DeBolt: *Write! Mathematics*
Kagan Cooperative Learning • 1 (800) WEE CO-OP

Evaluate It!

Name _____ Date _____

Directions: Fill in the topic in the box below. Write how you feel about the topic. Be prepared to share your evaluation with teammates.

How I feel about _____ .
topic

Write an evaluation of the topic. _____

_____

_____

_____

_____

_____

_____

_____

_____

_____

_____

_____

_____

_____

_____

_____

_____

_____

_____

_____

Part III

Cooperative Learning Structures

The directions regarding the structures used in the writing activities were specific for that activity. In this section of the book, you will find a more general description of the structures, one which may help you see how you can apply it in other ways in your classroom.

Dr. Spencer Kagan's book *Cooperative Learning* is the definitive resource and guide to cooperative learning structures. He has designed and refined over one hundred cooperative learning strategies, each one carefully planned to include the principles of cooperative learning. Those principles are:

- **Positive Interdependence**
- **Individual Accountability**
- **Equal Participation**
- **Simultaneous Interaction**

Using cooperative learning structures helps you achieve success with cooperative learning because the basic principles to successful cooperative learning are "built-in." The marvelous thing about the structures is that they are content-free. If you use an activity from this book involving Think-Pair-Share or RoundRobin with writing content, you can use these cooperative structures equally well with any content. From kindergarten to graduate school, from astrophysics to plumbing repair, cooperative learning structures are helpful tools to build effective learning experiences.

Virginia DeBolt: *Write! Mathematics*
Kagan Cooperative Learning • 1 (800) WEE CO-OP

105

Structure 1

Do-What-I-Write

Students write a description of a process or procedure, then switch papers to have a partner "do what the written description says." Do-What-I-Write develops strong writing skills as students must accurately describe the process.

Students write a definition or description of something, perhaps a graph or a timeline; or they write the steps of a process, perhaps long division. They exchange papers with someone who uses the writing to create or do what was described. Omissions, unclear or confusing wording, and other communication problems can be identified and changed through this process. Students become aware of the importance of precise language.

Structure 2

Find-Someone-Who...

Students circulate through the classroom looking for someone who possesses the needed information. Find-Someone-Who is a fun and energizing way for students to share information.

In Find-Someone-Who, students search the room for someone who possesses the needed information or material. As a classbuilding activity, students typically are given a handout with instructions such as: find someone who likes your favorite TV show or someone who has a pet. The search can be as specific as you want. For example, "Find-Someone-Who has an equation which equals 87 taped to their sleeve."

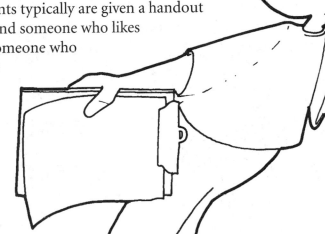

Since students must leave their desks and move around, here are a few hints for classroom management.

1. Search silently. If talking is a must, speak quietly.
2. Use nonverbal signals such as raised hands when looking for a match with someone.
3. Specify that each person may be used only once for filling in names on the answer sheet. This insures interactions between students stay brief and focused.

Virginia DeBolt: *Write! Mathematics*
Kagan Cooperative Learning • 1 (800) WEE CO-OP

107

Formations

Students use their bodies to create a formation related to the topic of study.

Formations is the penultimate bodily/kinesthetic learning experience. In Formations, students use their bodies to create answers. Bodies can form numbers, equations, symbols, processes, actions, graphs or patterns. Formations can be done in pairs, teams of four or as a whole class. Students can be allowed to plan their formation, or can be called upon without warning to, "With no talking, you four form the formula for finding the area of a circle."

Virginia DeBolt: *Write! Mathematics*
Kagan Cooperative Learning • 1 (800) WEE CO-OP

4S Brainstorming

Students each fulfill a role as they quickly brainstorm ideas as a team. 4S Brainstorming is an effective way to generate a range of creative ideas.

In teams of four, each student is assigned a role for the brainstorming session:
• **Speed Captain** - Applies time pressure. Creativity increases with speed.
• **Sergeant Support** - Encourages all ideas. Students contribute more when ideas are praised.
• **Sultan of Silly** - Encourages silly ideas and off-the-wall thinking. Promotes creative ideas.
• **Synergy Guru** - Encourages building on ideas.

One student can record all the team's ideas or students can take turns recording each new idea.

Virginia DeBolt: *Write! Mathematics*
Kagan Cooperative Learning • 1 (800) WEE CO-OP

109

Jigsaw

Students are each responsible for learning part of the material then sharing it with teammates. Jigsaw creates strong positive interdependence.

Jigsaw is a division of labor structure. A team is divided so that each teammate is responsible for one part of the material. The materials is usually divided into four parts. Students meet with others who are assigned the same material and work together to learn the material and plan how to present the material to teammates. Teammates are reunited and each student teaches teammates his or her part of the learning material.

Virginia DeBolt: *Write! Mathematics*
Kagan Cooperative Learning • 1 (800) WEE CO-OP

Pair Discussion

Students pair up to discuss any topic. Pair Discussion provides an intimate setting that promotes active discussion and listening.

Pair Discussion is simply two students pairing up for a brief time during which they discuss the matter under study. They might discuss the best way to do something, the best answer to a question, the steps in a process, or the meaning of a vocabulary word.

Pair Project

Students work together with a partner to complete a project. Pairs provide students the opportunity to collaborate, yet are small enough to maximize participation.

In Pair Project, two students pair up to work on an assigned project. The project can involve any type of pair work: creating products, doing research, solving problems, conducting experiments, inventing new machines. It is a good idea to create a project that neither student could do alone or to structure the project so that both students must contribute. This way, students are both accountable for their contribution and no one student can do all the work.

Virginia DeBolt: Write! Mathematics
Kagan Cooperative Learning • 1 (800) WEE CO-OP

111

Pairs Present

Pairs present their project with another pair, team, or the class. Pairs Present is an excellent way for students to share information with classmates and hone their presentation skills.

When two students have worked together on a project, assignment or experiment and have a product or results to share with the class, use a Pairs Present. The two should participate equally in the presentation, and in some way be held individually accountable for knowing all the information involved in the assignment.

RallyTable

In pairs, students take turns writing. RallyTable is a quick and easy way to generate and record ideas or write pair papers. The turn-taking ensures equal participation.

RallyTable is the pair alternative to RoundTable. Pairs share a common piece of paper, which they hand back and forth, each contributing in turn. Math examples to use Rallytable might be: "Come up with a list of everything you know about denominators, taking turns writing each fact." Or, "Write a paragraph on what you know about denominators, taking turns writing each sentence."

RoundRobin

Each student, in turn, shares with teammates. Roundrobin is an easy way to have students share any information with teammates in a format that ensures equal participation.

RoundRobin is simply speaking in turn within teams. For example, students can share how they feel about space exploration or can read their papers on space exploration to teammates. Many conditions can be attached to RoundRobin to make it achieve the results desired. For example, each person must speak for thirty seconds and no longer; or each person must quickly para-phrase (or praise) the previous person's comments before making their own; or each person must offer something new to the RoundRobin.

Virginia DeBolt: *Write! Mathematics*
Kagan Cooperative Learning • 1 (800) WEE CO-OP

113

RoundTable

In teams, students take turns writing. Roundtable is a great way to generate a list of ideas or to write team papers. The turn-taking ensures equal participation.

RoundTable is a written RoundRobin. Ideas, answers, or any type of contribution is made as the paper is passed around the table. RoundTable is an excellent structure for brainstorming and generating lists, especially if it is done quickly. For example, "List as many elements as you can." RoundTable also works well for writing as a team. Each student must participate in the team writing task. For example, "Write a brief description of the Periodic Table. Take turns writing each sentence."

Virginia DeBolt: *Write! Mathematics*
Kagan Cooperative Learning • 1 (800) WEE CO-OP

Send-A-Problem

Students generate questions and send them to other teams to solve. Send-A-Problem is an effective way to review learning materials and practice team problem-solving skills.

Each student writes a question or problem on a card. For review, have students write high-consensus questions for which there is a clear correct answer. Send-A-Problem can also be used with higher-level thinking questions that promote team discussion on the topic. Students check their questions or problems with teammates. If there is total consensus, the answer is written on the back of the card. (No answer is needed for higher-level thinking questions as there is usually no right or wrong answer.) Questions can also be written together as a team on a sheet of paper with the answers on the back or on a separate answer key. When teams have completed their questions or problems, they send them to another team to solve.

Student One reads the first problem aloud to teammates. The team works together to answer the problem. Problems can also be solved in pairs. Students check their answers by flipping over the card or checking with the key. If the team disagrees with the answer, they can work with the sending team to solve the discrepancy. Student Two reads the next card and the process is repeated until all the problems have been read and answered.

After the team has solved all problems or after a determined amount of time has passed, teams send the problems to another team to answer.

Simultaneous Chalkboard Share

A representative from each team simultaneously records the team's answer or idea on the chalkboard to share with the class. Simultaneous Chalkboard Share promotes information sharing among teams while saving valuable time.

Just as students benefit from sharing questions, answers and ideas within teams, teams can benefit by sharing with other teams. Teams can build on each other's ideas; an idea shared may trigger a whole new direction for exploration or spark new ideas for discussion. A representative from each team simultaneously records the team's answer or idea on a designated area of the chalkboard. Representatives can be team selected, or you can select each team's representative by announcing a student number, "Student Threes, please record your team's answer on the chalkboard." In a brief amount of time and with little interruption to the teamwork, all teams have access to each other's ideas or answers.

Virginia DeBolt: *Write! Mathematics*
Kagan Cooperative Learning • 1 (800) WEE CO-OP

Simultaneous RoundTable

In teams, students simultaneously write down an idea, then pass the paper for a teammate to record the next idea. In Simultaneous RoundTable, all students are actively participating as they simultaneously make contributions to the team's paper.

In Simultaneous RoundTable, each teammates pulls out a sheet of paper. They each record the first idea or sentence on the paper, then pass the paper clockwise. Teammates read the information on the paper, make a contribution, then pass it clockwise again. When completed, each team has four papers loaded with ideas or four different writings on a topic or on different, related topics. Simultaneous RoundTable can also be used to edit each other's work. Often, a set length of time is determined by the teacher. Students pass papers when you call, "Pass."

Team Discussion

Students discuss any topic as a team. Team Discussion is a simple, unstructured platform for students to share their ideas with teammates.

The teacher announces the topic to discuss. Discussion topics are usually open-ended with no right or wrong answers. For example, "Who is the most important mathematician?" Following the Team Discussion, select one student from several teams share their ideas with the entire class.

Structure 16

Team Project

Students work together as a team to complete a team project. Team Projects provide students a great deal of autonomy as they work cooperatively toward a common goal.

The teacher announces the team project. Each team may have a unique project or all teams may work on the same project. Projects can involve any type of teamwork: creating products, doing research, solving problems, composing a song, conducting experiments, coordinating a dance or movement. Without any structure, students may run into complications with a project. One or two students may do all of the work while the others do not contribute at all. To avoid this pitfall, try one or more of the following ideas:

• **Assign Roles** - Assign each student a role specific to the project. As a class, brainstorm and have students record "Things to Do" and "Things to Say" to fulfill each role. Some generic roles you may use include: Checker, Cheerleader, Coach, Encourager, Gatekeeper, Materials Monitor, Praiser, Question Commander, Quiet Captain, Recorder, Reflector, Taskmaster.

• **Divide the Work** - Divide the work of the project or have students divide the work so that everyone must participate.

• **Limit the Resources** - By limiting who can use which resources, students depend on each other for completing the project.

• **Individual Papers or Tests** - Have students each turn in their own paper on the topic or be responsible for their own learning. Do not use group grades for team projects.

Team Sort

Students work as a team to sort items or information into a predetermined system. Team Sort develops classification, categorization and sorting skills.

Working together as a team, students sort items into given categories or into a categorization system like a Venn diagram, two by two matrix, or a ranking ladder. The items for sorting can be generated by a team brainstorming session or can be provided. Students take turns placing items into the categorization system. When teams are done sorting, they can share or compare their resulting product with another team, or post their work for the class to see.

In Team Sort, also called Structured Sort, the categorization system is provided; in Unstructured Sort, students make up their own categorization systems.

Sample categorization systems:

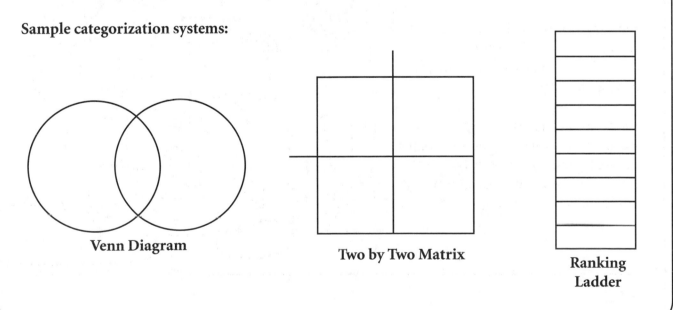

Venn Diagram

Two by Two Matrix

Ranking Ladder

Teams Present

Teams share their project with another team or with the class. Teams Present is a great way to practice presentation skills and disseminate information.

Following an activity or project in which the teams have worked to make a product or demonstrate an idea, have them present their work to another team or to the class. Presenting to one other team has the advantage of more active participation and a distinct time advantage. For each team to do a five-minute presentation to the class, with eight teams would take about 40 minutes. Of the 40 minutes, students are active presenters for five minutes and passive viewers for 35 minutes. Teams can present to one other team and watch one other team's five-minute presentation in just 10 minutes, during all of which they are active presenters or viewers. In the same amount of time as a class presentation, teams can share their presentation and view one other team's presentation four times. Repeated practice allows students the opportunity to hone their presentation skills. Presenting to the whole class has the advantage of a larger audience and the advantage of every student getting the opportunity to see every team's presentation.

Regardless of whether students present to one other team, to several teams, or to the whole class, it is still important to make sure each student is individually accountable for his or her own contribution. Students can be held accountable by each presenting part of the information, turning in a paper on the presentation, or being held responsible for all material in the presentation.

Virginia DeBolt: *Write! Mathematics*
Kagan Cooperative Learning • 1 (800) WEE CO-OP

Team Word Web

Students work in teams to create a web of ideas and details on a given topic. Word Webs promote visual thinking and visually depict the interrelations of the learning material.

To make word webs in teams, give each student a different colored marker and each team a large sheet of butcher paper. Word webs can also be made on smaller paper. The main topic of the word web is written in a rectangle in the center of the paper. Students do a RoundTable, adding core concepts sprouting from the main topics, circling the core concepts in the ovals. Then, students have a free-for-all, adding as many supporting details as possible and making connections where appropriate. Encourage students to suspend judgment and to quickly write down and integrate everything that comes to mind.

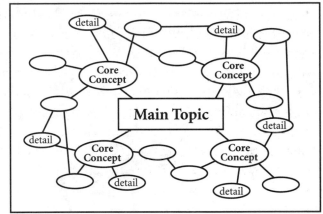

Have students add illustrations, symbols, bridges, and graphics to make mind maps.

Virginia DeBolt: *Write! Mathematics*
Kagan Cooperative Learning • 1 (800) WEE CO-OP

121

ThinkPad Brainstorming

Students generate a number of ideas on a given topic, each on a separate thinkpad slip and share their ideas with teammates. ThinkPad Brainstorming promotes creative thinking.

In ThinkPad Brainstorming, students work individually, recording their brainstormed ideas on thinkpad slips, small sheets of paper or cards. After a period of time or after students have generated enough ideas on a topic, students share their ideas in a RoundRobin. Teammates work together to see if they can build on ideas generated or come up with new and even better ideas. The ideas that are generated can be easily sorted and categorized. See Team Sort.

Think-Pair-Share

After a question or topic is announced by the teacher, students "Think" about the question, "Pair" up with a partner to discuss the question, then some students are selected to "Share" their ideas with the class. Think-Pair-Share is a simple and powerful technique for developing and sharing ideas.

The teacher poses a question for the class to think about. Think-Pair-Share works best with low-consensus, thinking questions to which there is not a right or wrong answer. For example, some questions to spark some interest on endangered species, "Some species are threatened with extinction. Should we let natural selection run its course, or should we intervene?" Or, "What are some things we could do to help protect the bald eagle?" Give students a good 10-15 seconds of think time. Then, have students pair up with another student on their team to share what they think. After students have shared their ideas, select a few students to share with the class their ideas, or their partner's ideas. Think-Pair-Share can be used several times in succession to follow a line of reasoning or more fully develop a concept with interrelated issues. Have students pair up with a different teammate with each new question.

1. Think

2. Pair

3. Share

Virginia DeBolt: *Write! Mathematics*
Kagan Cooperative Learning • 1 (800) WEE CO-OP

123

Structure 22

Think-Write-Pair-Share

In this variation of Think-Pair-Share, students write down their own ideas before they pair up to discuss them with a partner. Think-Write-Pair-Write allows students to more fully develop their own ideas before sharing them.

After the think time, students write down their own ideas. This allows more reflective students and students who develop their thinking through writing explore the question or issue in more detail before they are asked to share their ideas with a partner. When students pair up, they read what they wrote to their partner, then discuss the issue more. The added writing component often leads to a richer pair discussion. Select a few students to share their writing, their partner's writing, or the ideas they discussed with the class.

1. Think

2. Write

3. Pair

4. Share

Think-Write-RoundRobin

After a question or topic is announced by the teacher, students "Think" about the question, "Write" down their ideas on the topic, then "RoundRobin" read their writing to teammates. Think-Write-RoundRobin allows students to develop their ideas on a topic, as well as hear the ideas of teammates.

The teacher announces a question to the class. Students are given 10-15 seconds of think time, then are instructed to write down their ideas. After ample writing time, students RoundRobin read their writing to teammates.

1. Think

2. Write

3. RoundRobin

Virginia DeBolt: *Write! Mathematics*
Kagan Cooperative Learning • 1 (800) WEE CO-OP

125

Write-What-I-Do

Students "write" what their partners "do." Write-What-I-Do develops communication and writing skills.

Group students in pairs. One student will record what the other student says aloud as he or she works through a problem step by step. The result will be a sequenced "list" of steps which the student working through the problem can use to write an explanation of the process. Students change roles after the first list is complete so that the student who previously recorded will now work and talk his or her way through a problem.

Virginia DeBolt: *Write! Mathematics*
Kagan Cooperative Learning • 1 (800) WEE CO-OP

Barrow, John D. *Pi in the Sky.* Clarendon Press, Oxford, 1992.

Bloom, Benjamin S., et al. *A Taxonomy of Educational Objectives: Handbook 1: Cognitive Domain.* Longman, New York, 1977.

Campbell, Linda, Campbell, Bruce and Dickinson, Dee. *Teaching and Learning Through Multiple Intelligences.* New Horizons for Learning, Stanwood, WA, 1992.

Cooney, Miriam P., C.S.C., ed. *Celebrating Women in Mathematics and Science.* National Council of Teachers of Mathematics, Weston, CA, 1996.

Countryman, Joan. *Writing to Learn Mathematics.* Heinemann, Portsmouth, NH 1992.

Cushman, Jean. *Do You Wanna Bet?* Clarion Books, New York, 1991.

DeBolt, Virginia. *Write! Cooperative Learning and the Writing Process.* Kagan Cooperative Learning, San Clemente, CA, 1994.

Gere, Anne Ruggles, ed. *Roots in the Sawdust: Writing to Learn across the Disciplines.* National Council of Teachers of English, Urbana, IL, 1985.

Historical Connections in Mathematics., Vol. I, II, and III. ISDN 1-881431-35-5, 1-881431-38-X, and 1-881431-49-5.

Humez, Alexander, et.al. *Zero to Lazy Eight.* Simon and Schuster, New York, 1993.

Markle, Sandra. *Math Mini Mysteries.* Atheneum, New York, 1993.

Kagan, Laurie, Kagan, Miguel, and Kagan Spencer. *Teambuilding.* Kagan Cooperative Learning, San Clemente, CA, 1997.

Kagan, Miguel, Robertson, Laurie and Kagan, Spencer. *Classbuilding.* Kagan Cooperative Learning, San Clemente, CA, 1995.

Kagan, Spencer. *Cooperative Learning.* Kagan Cooperative Learning, San Clemente, CA, 1994.

Virginia DeBolt: *Write! Mathematics*
Kagan Cooperative Learning • 1 (800) WEE CO-OP

127

Bibliography (cont)

Kagan, Spencer and Kagan, Miguel. *Advanced Cooperative Learning: Playing with Elements.* Kagan Cooperative Learning, San Clemente, CA, 1994.

Kagan, Spencer and Kagan, Miguel. *Multiple Intelligences: Teaching With, For, and About MI.* Kagan Cooperative Learning, San Clemente, CA, 1998.

Paulos, John Allen. *Innumeracy.* Hill and Wang, New York, 1989.

Rico, Gabriele. *Writing the Natural Way: Using Right-Brain Techniques to Release Your Expressive Powers.* Tarcher, Los Angeles, CA 1983.

Shaw, Vanston. *Communitybuilding.* Kagan Cooperative Learning, San Clemente, CA, 1992.

Tankard, James W. *The Statistical Pioneers.* Schenkman Publishing Co., Cambridge, Mass., 1984.

Tompkins, Gale. *Teaching Writing: Balancing Process and Product.* Macmillan, New York, 1994.

Van Cleave, Janice. *Geometry for Every Kid.* Wiley and Sons, New York, 1994.

Zinsser, William. *On Writing Well: An Informal Guide to Writing Nonfiction.* Harper Perennial, New York, 1994.

128

Virginia DeBolt: *Write! Mathematics*
Kagan Cooperative Learning • 1 (800) WEE CO-OP

About the Author

Virginia DeBolt has been teaching for thirty years in Colorado, New Mexico and Texas. She is currently teaching English at Murchison Middle School in Austin, Texas. She has worked with all ages from kindergarten to adult, but enjoys most the opportunity to work with other teachers and share ideas about writing and cooperative learning. She is interested in publishing students' writing on the internet and is creating a web home page for her school. Her personal home page can be viewed at http://www.flash.net/~vdebolt.

More Books by Virginia

Write! Cooperative Learning and the Writing Process

Three methods to make your students better writers: Have them 1) Write! 2) Write! and 3) Write some more. You receive ready-to-use writing lessons in each of the writing domains: imaginative, functional, communication, non-fiction/reporting, and opinion making. Cooperative learning structures are used at each of the stages of the writing process: prewriting, writing, proofing and editing, conferring and rewriting, and publishing. Includes practical management tips, references, resources, and ideas for evaluating students' writing with portfolios, holistic scoring, primary trait scoring, analytic, self evaluation, and peer evaluation.

Write! Across the Curriculum Book Series

Move beyond drill and kill. Teach for understanding. Integrate writing across the curriculum! When students write in science, social studies and mathematics, they delve deeply into content and issues, their thinking is clarified and they obtain a deeper understanding and appreciation for the content. Writing makes the content accessible to your verbal/linguistic students. Each book includes 36 multiple intelligences, cooperative writing activities with ready-to-use reproducible activity pages, and brief descriptions of dozens of strategies. Teammates work cooperatively on these writing activities. Writing activities are a perfect way to start the class, introduce a new concept, end the unit, or use as a sponge activity.

Write! Mathematics
Includes activities like writing the steps of solving a problem, composing word problems, restating definitions, and translating the language of math

Write! Science
Includes activities like keeping a science log, defining science concepts, writing how something works, prioritizing world problems, coming up with a new invention.

Write! Social Studies
Includes activities like writing the correspondence of two historical characters, publishing and sharing political cartoons, discussing and writing about famous historical quotations.

Available from Kagan Cooperative Learning

Virginia DeBolt: *Write! Mathematics*
Kagan Cooperative Learning • 1 (800) WEE CO-OP

129

Notes